GLENVIEW
PROHIBITION
BOOTLEGGERS & BOONDOGGLES

JILL RUSCHLI CRANE

Foreword by Rick Kogan

THE
History
PRESS

Published by The History Press
Charleston, SC
www.historypress.com

Front cover, top: Meier's Tavern. *From* Glenview, the First Centennial; *bottom*: John Hoffman Hotel and Tavern, built in 1867. *From* Glenview, the First Centennial.
Back cover: Matt Hoffman (*far left*) during his iceman days. *Courtesy George R. Pinkowski.*

First published 2022

Manufactured in the United States

ISBN 9781467149280

Library of Congress Control Number: 2022937939

This is dedicated to all who ever gathered in Glenview's drinking establishments, from the 1830s, when Glenview was just getting its feet wet, to present times. Speaking of wet feet, this book is also dedicated to everyone who ever dipped a toe in Roosevelt Pool, the ultimate drink, where generations of us lived our entire summers.

Cheers!

CONTENTS

Foreword, by Rick Kogan   7
Acknowledgements   11
Introduction   15

1. A Hard-Drinking Town—Not!   17
2. Talk About Your Raw Deals   31
3. What Prohibition?   47
4. Shocked, Shocked, Drinking's Going On   67
5. It's All About the Good Hooch   95
6. Happy Days Are Here Again   118

Notes   143
Bibliography   151
About the Author   159

FOREWORD

I am a city kid, my earliest memories filled with concrete. I cannot remember the first time I learned that there were such things called suburbs, later still when I ventured there with my parents, who had many friends scattered about the area.

The North Shore was my most frequently visited territory, and most of it seemed like some sort of enchanted land of big trees and wide lawns and large homes. I would, over the years, come to know that there were stories too, the type that make interesting cocktail party conversations.

But none of that prepared me for the excitement and enlightenment I got from devouring this book by Jill Crane. This marvelous and incisive book is meticulously and energetically researched and written with a sparkling and distinctive style.

There is something fascinating on virtually every page, such as learning early on that the history of Glenview's taverns goes back to the 1820s. That was fine, I suppose, if you lived in the area because, as Crane writes, "stagecoach travel was no picnic." Depending on the weather, it could take as long as three days to get from Chicago to Milwaukee.

Things would, of course, get easier, and by the twentieth century, the suburb's Waukegan Road was "a parade of roadhouses, saloons, bars, inns and dance halls." As Crane tells us, they were once "part and parcel of the old family-owned hostels, catering to the weary long-distance horse or stagecoach travelers." By the early '20s, they "welcomed carloads of people from Chicago and the North Shore suburbs." Automobiles were the rage now, and people were looking for reasons and places to drive. These swarms grew as Prohibition wore on, especially in Glenview.

This made of Glenview what Crane rightly calls "a contradiction," since, while being a farm town priding itself on "providing safe neighborhoods to raise healthy children and good businesses," it was also a center for "blind pigs, speakeasies, roadhouses, nightclubs, cocktail lounges, saloons, taverns, cafés, resorts, beer gardens and restaurants, which made many people rich, some angry, some sad and some dead."

There is much trouble and mystery peppering this book's pages. And you'll encounter such big-city "businessmen" as Johnny Torrio, Bugs Moran and Al Capone.

But there is also fun, as when Crane pulls from the past this delightful exchange that resulted from one of the suburb's then three police officers nabbing a driver for speeding on what was called Death Curve on Waukegan Road.

The police officer told the judge, "He took the curve on high, Your Honor."

"I always do things fast," said the offender. The judge replied, "See how fast you can dig up fifteen dollars and costs."

There may indeed still be some old-timers who can recall the bawdy times and such places as the Garden of Allah, which "brought a new delicacy into Glenview boundaries in the fall of 1923." Crane writes that the nightclub "looked like something out of the Hollywood movies....Built for $200,000 on the land where Lyons School stands today, the Garden of Allah was an island of pure paradise in the form of a cabaret...decorated like a Turkish villa replete with arched doorways, domed hallways, velvet drapes and luscious, private alcoves. It was said 'the kitchen was so big you could turn around in it with a Model T Ford.'"

My favorite of the bygone places is certainly the Villa Venice, built on the banks of the Des Plaines River by Albert Bouch, a native of the city of, of all places, Nice, France. It had been "superbly landscaped into gardens such as no roadhouse ever boasted before." It had gondolas, good food and three shows a night. It was opened in 1924 and was taken over decades later by a group of investors, among them a "silent" partner who was mob boss Sam Giancana.

It was he who managed to, as Crane puts it, employ "ladies of the evening [who] were available for gentlemen who desired feminine company." He also persuaded some pals to visit. Late in 1962, the spot had Frank Sinatra and members of his Rat Pack performing seven nights of shows. But from there, "Villa Venice went downhill, reduced to a catering hall. New owners took over in 1965, and in March 1967, it was destroyed by, guess what?" Crane writes. "Another one of those mysterious fires."

I can only be grateful that some of the Glenview past remains, and what does not, Crane brings gloriously back to life with you-are-there style.

I was lucky enough to have the pleasure of Matty's Wayside Inn until it died in flames in 2009. But there has long been and remains another suburban hamburger oasis, which Crane explores in a fascinating section: "That Age-Old Glenview Question: Which Hackney's Came First? Harms or Lake?"

And there is also Meier's Tavern. I have—to my great good fortune— been there and continue to go. I have even written about it for the *Tribune*, saying, in part, "When it opened it was like a lot of other roadhouses that dotted the suburbs. But most have vanished, replaced by burger-chicken-pizza franchises. Meier's now seems almost a curiosity, but a glorious one."

I suppose I could now tell you about the Roosevelt Pool or some of the other things I discovered in this delightful book. But one of the great treats of exploring the past is to make the discoveries on your own. So, have at it.

— Rick Kogan

ACKNOWLEDGEMENTS

Since this story started thirty years before my birth, my first thank-you goes to my dear old dad, who exposed old family tales, followed by "Bill, *shhh!*" from my mother. My grandmother, a Glenview flapper of sorts, also requires a thank-you for her memories of those days when she met my grandfather, a Glenview bootlegger. My cousin Karen Kelly Bohlke detailed stories her flapper mother and bootlegger father told her about the whiskey trafficking (among other things) that went on in Glenview during the Roaring Twenties. I have immeasurable gratitude to another newfound relative (thanks to Ancestry.com), Joe Foster, who went above and beyond as he found news articles and pictures of my great-grandfather Ed Kelly and his antics in Half Day. It is them that I thank first.

With acknowledgement, gratitude and a certain sweetness, I can't thank George R. enough for our conversations that developed from his talks with his grandmother, wife of Matt Hoffman. George passed away shortly before this book was published, so there is a true sadness that he didn't get to see his research in print. His energy in uncovering the facts surrounding his grandfather's tragic death at Hackney's on Harms gave my book real teeth and the effective history of our town during the dry years. His generosity in supplying me with stacks of research materials, including additional Richard L. Schneider notes, was invaluable. His own manuscript about his grandfather, "Biography of the Gross Point Bootlegger," details significant aspects of Matt Hoffman's life, which gave my accounts true breath. I also want to throw a shout-out to his cousin Terry Schneider Mikos for her help on the Schneider family tree.

This never would have gotten off the ground without the upbeat charm of Liz Hebson, granddaughter of the original owners of the Lake Avenue Tavern, forerunner of Hackney's on Lake. She suggested it might be fun to discover some of the secrets bound up in Glenview during Prohibition. Sally Masterson Landri gave me a priceless family letter about the history of Hackney's, written by Frank Engels, son of Frank and Betty Engels. Thank you to Mary Hebson Corby, Geege and Elaine Masterson and Mary Masterson Welch. Also, thank you to the myriad writers in the local press who provided decades-long supplies of articles about the Hackney's events and family, as well as other saloons and taverns in the area. Liz Hebson's grandmother was a friend of my grandmother's, who lived across the street in those Prohibition times and made these histories more real.

Thank you to John J. Binder (*Al Capone's Beer Wars*), who recommended Daniel Russell's master's thesis from 1931, "The Road House: A Study of Commercialized Amusements in the Environs of Chicago," at the Chicago History Museum. He also sent me papers written by Richard L. Schneider about Matt Hoffman, as did Siobhan Heraty, curator at the Des Plaines History Center.

Exploring old Glenview saloons and their origins began with my long friendship with Andrew Karas, owner of Gusto in Glenview, who wanted to share his bar with a little Prohibition history. I researched pictures of old Glenview saloons, added a few explanations and hung them where his patrons were intrigued, which offered me another reason to write this book.

My dearest gratitude goes to Gus Pappas and Lori Schanmier at Meier's Tavern. Their knowledge of the history of the Meier family, as we spent time talking at the bar, brought the old days to light. Their pictures hopefully help the reader find the same light. Sally Masterson Landri confirmed her dad's appreciation for the pony rink at the old tavern "so he could spend more time with his kids." I also appreciate Tommy Reece of Old Times Pony Rides in Ironville, Missouri. He helped me understand how a pony wheel works and which horses are the most rideable for the little ones. Another shout-out to Kevin Middleton at Grandpa's Place for trying to help me fill in their history. It was at Grandpa's Place that I was lucky enough to meet Chance Heubner, a curious young gentleman who was awarded his citizenship badge for Boy Scouts by writing a project on Glenview history, based on his daily encounter with the giant picture of Lang's Tavern, found on the lower floor at Grandpa's. What a treat to see young people interested in the old days. Thank you to Michelle Sifuentes of the Ontario Museum of History and Art and Anna Campbell from Elk Cove Vineyards for their help and pictures of wine bricks.

Thank you, Rachel Ramirez of the Wilmette History Museum, for her enthusiasm and, more importantly, hard work when helping me to find some of the pictures and research involving the pesky four-mile limit in the early years of Gross Point. Thank you, Ashley DeAngeles, operations supervisor at the Grove. Thank you to Michael McCarty, Jena Johnson and Amy Wille of the Glenview Park District for putting me in touch with Bob Quill, former Glenview Park District superintendent, whose prolific memories and emails practically wrote the entire section about Roosevelt Pool. Also, thank you, Doug Jones from Glenview, for your memories of the early days of Roosevelt Pool.

Thank you to Judith Joslyn Hughes from the Northbrook Historical Society, Beverly Dawson and Susan Johns from the Glenview History Center. Thank you very much to my two new friends at the Glenview Library, Kimberly Schlarman and Natalie Bowling, who patiently handled my inexperience with the microfilm machine and approved an extra hour or two of overtime for me during the middle of Covid.

For stories on the Villa Venice not found in Glenview historical books, my gratitude goes to the website Under Every Tombstone (undereverytombstone. blogspot.com), where Jim Craig from Evanston wrote an outstanding article, overloaded with photos, about the noted Albert "Papa" Bouche. He turned me on to Richard Larson, who wrote a short book on the Villa Venice, as well as other documentaries, his new one being *The Other Side of Capone*. A blurb from the 1927 *Chicagoan* presented firsthand information about the "ultimate" restaurant and showplace.

The Garden of Allah was well detailed in a small brochure by Glenview's Ken Faig stored at the Glenview Public Library. Learning about the Garden of Allah on Sunset in Los Angeles was a real treat when I came across a great article by Kirk Silsbee in *GQ* magazine.

Special thanks and a ton of well-deserved gratitude go to Rick Kogan for his consummate foreword that put a great spin on the start of this book. Speaking of friends, my thanks also go to Bob Leopold, Glenview Art League artist and great supporter of this book, and his friend Jim, who spent endless time and effort on cover art possibilities.

An enormous thank-you befits Elias Savada, director of the Motion Picture Information Service, who was indispensable in educating and assisting me in the interminable vagueness of copyright issues. This book would have taken years to write but for the website newspapers.com, which was essential in finding news articles, especially from the *Chicago Tribune*. I think I read every page of the "World's Greatest Paper" from 1919 to 1936.

Certain websites were such a boon to me, and I appreciate their assistance, especially those that gave me pictures: Dave Alexander at Legends of America (www.legendsofamerica.com), Claire White at the Mob Museum (themobmuseum.org), the Library of Congress (www.loc.gov) and, most notably, Neal Gale at the Digital Research Library of Illinois History (drloihjournal.blogspot.com), who is saving Illinois history one story at a time. His blog was indispensable, illuminating and interesting. Gangsters Inc. (www.gangstersinc.org), University of Illinois (illinois.edu/research) and, of course, Wikipedia were awesome.

A huge thank you to Ben Gibson and Caroline Rodrigues from Arcadia Publishing/The History Press, and a very special thank you to John Kim at Glenview MotoPhoto for his help in getting the images in order.

Finally, my most endearing gratitude and love go to Bob Borgstrom, who helped me decide to do this project, picked me up when I wanted to quit and edited every word with his red pencil.

INTRODUCTION

One gauzy summer night in 2020, Liz Hebson and I shared a glass of wine on the patio at Hackney's on Lake and watched the sun set over the little white building just yards west. In 1924, it was the Lake Street Tavern and home to Liz's grandparents and the ancestor to all the Hackney restaurants.

"The stories those walls could tell," Liz said. I agreed. Our grandmothers were friends, and my Nana relived her Roaring Twenties at my childhood kitchen table. "Everybody had a tavern and sold beer." Local boys—including my grandfather and great-uncle—happily transported whiskey for a lot of extra bucks. As a little one, my mother even sat on the knee of the infamous Bugs Moran. These were the campy tales that prompted me to write this book.

I learned Glenview was a small, upstanding farming town, guided by conscientious leaders and citizens, humbly proud of the principled village they built. Prohibition eventually put a dent in that rationale. In the North Shore suburbs, Northwestern University was established in 1851. The nine Methodists who purchased the lakefront property wrote into their charter that no alcoholic beverages would be allowed within four miles of the future Big Ten franchise. In 1909, that little rule decimated Gross Point, a small town of 750 people and fifteen bars located between Glenview and Wilmette. A thirst (if you will) was born out of a wildly successful propaganda campaign that shut down the manufacture, sale and delivery of alcoholic beverages for thirteen years, starting in 1920 with national Prohibition.

Since the new law could not legislate morality, the founding of Glenview blind pigs, taverns, saloons, cabarets and nightclubs surged. Many of these roadhouses sprouted from living rooms and kitchens of local folks who carried on years of habits with families and friends. As touted in the 1939 movie *Roaring Twenties*, "It was one thing to pass a law, another to make it work. There'll always be guys wanting to drink—they'll enforce *that* law." People like Frank and Betty Engels, Bill Fisher, Frank and Anna Meier and many more met Glenview's needs, catering to the local beer-drinking culture and waves of people from Chicago and the dry North Shore. Most people just wanted a beer with their meal.

By the end of Prohibition, five hundred "ice cream parlors," roadhouses, bars, nightclubs and eating establishments garnished Waukegan Road between Chicago and Lake County. These establishments, however illegal they might have been, helped to brighten the financial picture in Glenview. Like others who built the small town, the average, everyday citizens marked this compelling and mysterious chapter in Glenview's history as they faced the issues during the dry era and the Great Depression. Unfortunately, before the decade was out, gangs enabled by Chicago's corrupt law enforcement and legislators exploited the Glenview entrepreneurs. Violence and fear exploded. Well-meaning people were victimized; some were killed.

Sadly, some people are hesitant to speak freely about the bootlegging activity in our small village. History should be about facts, and many times facts are sympathetic. George R. Pinkowski, the grandson of Matt Hoffman, the neighborhood beer brewer, learned the details of this terrible time. He, too, had a kitchen table seat next to his grandmother, the widow of Matt Hoffman. She confided her secrets to this curious youngster, and he confided in me. (Well, not confided, as he wanted this story known.) When Prohibition finally ended, Glenview businesses exhaled a sigh of relief. Then came the New Deal, a policy that most of the citizens of Glenview felt to be the epitome of socialism. Out of this came the Civilian Conservation Corps, which revitalized young men and families with hard work, resulting in the reconditioning of the Skokie Lagoons. Moving past the socialistic fears, the Glenview Park administrators weren't about to shuck off a good deal. A Public Works Administration project, "the beach away from the lake," was planned with the support of decades-long endeavors of "Glenview Days." On July 4, 1940, the ultimate "drink," Roosevelt Pool, opened, setting the stage for the postwar boom and Glenview's soaring growth.

CHAPTER I

A HARD-DRINKING TOWN—NOT!

Glenview wasn't a hard-drinking town any more than Chicago was run by a convent full of Franciscan nuns. No one had time to drink or even the inclination in this close-knit town of 760 farmers,[1] landscapers and bricklayers. Then there were the merchants, railroad workers, phone operators and barbers. Their work ethic was strong and, for a pocket-sized village incorporated only twenty-one years earlier, induced these few hundred people to build schools, roads and laws. Drinking was, indeed, part of their culture, especially beer drinking, but so were dancing and families and friends who met for picnics on Sundays and German Oktoberfest, which took over every September. There were those hearty men who hung out in a few roadhouses trading farming advice, exchanging gossip and news and, of course, enduring the never-ending political squabbles.

This story accommodates some of the tales of Glenview businesses, focusing on the roadhouses and bars, up to the launch of the best watering hole in Glenview: Roosevelt Pool.

THE STAGECOACH PLOWS THROUGH WEST NORTHFIELD[2]

A brief history about the taverns in Glenview (then called West Northfield) begins in the mid-1830s, when travel by stagecoach, a rough ride in a rudimentary open cart, was primarily used to deliver mail. William Lovejoy, Glenview's first stage driver, dropped off the mail at the west end on Pottawatomi Trail, which would become Milwaukee Trace. The stop was just south of what would become Glenview Road. Every fifteen to eighteen miles, tired horses were exchanged along with, eventually, passengers. These stagecoach stops often began as cramped homes where the families fed the travelers and boarded them overnight, if necessary.

In 1845, Frink and Walker invested in four-horse post coaches and ran daily rides with minimal stops at taverns or inns, which grew to serve as town halls, trading posts and sometimes even churches. For some people, usually the wagon master, the most immediate need for getting off the stagecoach was the actual tavern, called a grog house or tippling house, a practice not appreciated by the women passengers.

Stagecoach travel was no picnic. Depending on the weather, it took two to three days to get from Chicago to Milwaukee. Typically, a stagecoach ran three times a week, carrying six people stuffed into a tight, bumpy cabin with valises, mail and supplies secured on top. In the winter, the only warmth provided to the crowded passengers was their body heat while they chugged along over frozen ruts on the narrow, winding trails. Spring brought floods, mud and stuck wagon wheels, so the passengers often had to climb out of their tight, sticky seats and push the coaches out of the muck after searching for rocks and broken limbs to use as levers. With incessant flies and mosquitoes and the oppressive heat, summer might have been the worst. Reaching the taverns or inns could be a welcome relief—or maybe not. Schedules were so erratic that food wasn't cooked until the passengers arrived, when the jingle of horse bells announced their arrival. Women and men often had to sleep in the same room for the overnighters.

In 1845, near Shermer and Glenview Roads (in those days, Telegraph and Lake Roads), Alex Turney opened a tavern and smithy. It's likely that in this tavern, a place where neighbors convened and bonded, conversation centered on the two new schools that were built that year, farmland for $7.50 an acre (up from $1.25 in 1833), the invention of the rotary printing press and the John Deere tractor. The town began to move east, and by the Gay Nineties, Waukegan Road had become the passage north out of Chicago.

GLENVIEW ROADHOUSES[3]

John Hoffman erected a three-story frame building on the southeast corner of Glenview and Waukegan Roads, providing his guests with a tavern and dining room on the first floor and sleeping and living quarters on the second and third floors. A white picket fence gave the inn a nice cozy look.

Crossing Glenview Road (called Lake Street at the time), north of Hoffman's place, a man could down a beer at William Haut's two-story inn in his saloon, and the lady could buy some goods at his general store. Haut had a little park for outdoor dances, Sunday family feasts and Oktoberfest in the summer. Haut built a ballroom upstairs, exploiting the dance craze, which could be accessed by a conspicuous entry on Waukegan Road. Everybody, of every age, flocked to his parties and socials. By the end of Prohibition, Waukegan Road going north would become a parade of more roadhouses, saloons, bars and other evening extravaganzas.

Across Waukegan Road from Haut's dance hall was a small commercial area like an old-time scene from Currier & Ives. The inn/saloon business was booming when John Lies built a two-story frame roadhouse featuring a thirty-by-fifty-foot bar facing the river's south wall. He filled in the space with

John Hoffman Hotel and Tavern, built in 1867. *From* Glenview, the First Centennial.

The Blue Heron is on the left, and William Haut's Inn is on the right. *Glenview History Center.*

a pool table and card tables. The river was about sixty feet wide yet only three or four feet deep. In the good old summertime, the river became a swimming hole and a place for fishing. In the winter, parents brought their children in sleds down the river. Living on the river also gave Lies a prosperous ice business. Once the river froze to a foot thick, the ice was cut into blocks, covered with sawdust and stored in his icehouse. Lies used his ice to cool barrels of beer, not crushing for highballs. It was a lucrative enterprise, probably because there were so many other practical needs for food cooling in the village.

Next to Lies Saloon, F.N. Hoffman had a general store. Farmers could bring in a sack of fresh cucumbers to Squire Dinghe's Pickles for a decent income. Christ Schall had a harness shop. Behind his harness shop was a little shack where Bob White lived. Well respected, tall and strong, White was from a good family but preferred living alone, growing his long white beard and drinking whenever he felt like it.

Bill Cummings bought this entire property at the end of the Gay Nineties; tore down the saloon, shops and shed; and built a grand modern restaurant he named the Blue Heron. Bill's place catered to the city people. A simple phone call to the restaurant resulted in chicken dinner upon the patron's arrival. For the folks in Glenview, the Blue Heron was a place to celebrate family milestones, civic affairs, business doings and fundraisers. It is unknown what happened to Bob White and his long white beard.

A word about the early geography of this intersection is that there wasn't one—an intersection, that is. Because of the river, Glenview Road didn't go straight through to Waukegan Road. This put the Blue Heron in the sweet little middle of a triangle bounded by Waukegan Road, River Drive and the end of Glenview Road.

From this part of Glenview Road, the only way to buggy to Haut's place was to turn left on a tiny little lane called River Drive. Even today, this one-block street runs southeast along the river and angles into Waukegan Road. Because of the river, a left turn at the end of River Drive provided a scary little curve on Waukegan Road. It wasn't quite so treacherous when

Left: The front of an advertising poster for the Blue Heron. *From* Glenview, the First Centennial.

Right: The back of the advertising poster for the Blue Heron. It's assumed the picture is of the Cummings family, but no other pictures of the family are available for comparison. *From* Glenview, the First Centennial.

horses were on the trot, but when Henry Ford multiplied the land with a million Model Ts, booze-driven roughriders learned the joy of high speeds at night with no lights. The little bend soon became known as the Death Curve. If one happened to get this far without veering into a ditch and wanted to continue north, a left turn on Waukegan would get the traveler back to Haut's place and beyond. The curve on Waukegan Road still exists, and it's a curiosity that one can drive the Waukegan Road straightaway for miles going south, and after the curve, Waukegan Road is just as straight going north.

In 1926, it was decided to connect the two Glenview Roads, which necessitated a rather unique architectural feat for the Blue Heron. Since half of the restaurant stood where the new road was being constructed, Cummings split his restaurant and moved half of it north enough to make way for the new main drag. To this day, the basement still extends under Glenview Road. It also accounts for the unusual door in the middle of a fireplace where the building faces Waukegan Road.

Even before the "connection" of the Glenview Roads, the railroad tracks outstretched the uptown a few blocks westward. In 1872, Sarah Hutchings donated land, and John Henley sold railroad rights-of-way to pave the way (so to speak) to construct a single rail line. The Chicago, Milwaukee and St. Paul Railroad now connected Glenview to Chicago, Techny, Shermerville and other towns, contributing more business to all the suburbs, as well as John Dilg's Glen View House on Glenview Road.

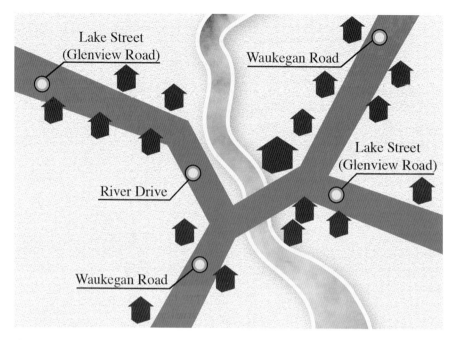

Above: Re-created map showing the Death Curve on Waukegan Road. The original (not shown) was hand drawn by Tomasine "Tommy" Allan, a teacher at the New School, and is from *Glenview, the First Centennial*. *Map redrawn by Caroline Rodrigues*.

Opposite: The Glen View House with its third floor before the fire that destroyed it. *Glenview History Center.*

Like any entrepreneur in any small town, John Dilg stretched himself to meet the community's needs. His saloon housed the Catholic church, the Masonic Hall, a dance hall and the village hall. In 1899, it was in his bar that Glenview became incorporated. The committee appointed its first constables, John Lies, William Haut and John Dilg, to maintain law and order. All three were saloon owners.

Across from Dilg's Inn stood the forerunner of the modern mall: Rugen Stores. Until it closed in 1978, this Glenview icon was better than Amazon. Arranged in several departments under one roof, it was the go-to from anything to everything. In the hardware department, one could find a simple screwdriver or John Deere riding tractor. The connecting department was a little grocery store. Vegetables and fruit were displayed in the front window. Shelves were filled with whatever groceries the lady needed and penny candies for the kiddos. Other departments included the new post office, an accounting office, a dry goods store and a shoe

store. Topping it all off were second-floor apartments, one of which was occupied by Fred Rugen and family, the proprietor of this entire giant accomplishment.

Behind Rugen Stores, along the railroad tracks, were the Chicago Telephone Company and what would become Hines's lumberyard. A block north, on Prairie Street, Lang's Tavern—which, after the Great War, became Rugen's Tavern—put a nice little nightcap on the neighborhood.

THE GREAT WAR

Sick of losing ships and Americans to German torpedoes, the United States reluctantly entered the Great War[4] in 1917. Over four million men were conscripted to fight. Before 1917, some American men had already headed off to Europe to "do their duty to fight and defend the principles necessary to keep world order." Many fought in the trenches, but some of the boys, such as Kiffen Rockwell and Eddie Rickenbacker, took to the skies in the French Lafayette Aviation Corps, as there was no American air corps at the time. Once the war began for the Americans, Herb Rugen and Joseph Sesterhenn crossed the pond for their commitment to stamp out fascism. Future bootlegger John "Andy" Andersen of the army's cavalry division was promoted to sergeant on his first day at war. He said the prodigious promotion came about because he was the only soldier who knew anything about horses. After a year and a half and the loss of 116,708 military personnel, the war was thankfully over.

EARLY ARMISTICE FOOLS AMERICA

Because of a misconstrued message when French officials asked German delegates to discuss armistice, a ceasefire was ordered at 3:00 p.m. French time on November 8, 1918. The dumbfounded (dumb being the operative word) operators on the receiving end of the message passed it on to the American Embassy, military bases and the public. A cablegram was sent to the War Department in Washington, D.C., which arrived at 9:00 a.m. eastern time the following day. From there, the message made its way to the United Press. Looking for more clarity, interpreters couldn't find the UP censors because they had already gone out to celebrate. The news was out. The war had ended!

Cities went nuts as they celebrated in "peace riots." The New York City mayor declared a public holiday. Barbers left their clients, half shaved, in their chairs as they rushed out to the streets. Signs appeared on doors: "Who can work on a day like this? Gone to Celebrate—Open Tomorrow." In Times Square, Enrico Caruso waved a flag and sang the national anthem from a second-floor window at the Knickerbocker Hotel.

In Washington, D.C., President Hoover appeared on the White House portico and waved his luncheon napkin to the crowds yelling his name. Nine navy planes performed loop de loops over the Capitol.

John "Andy" Andersen, future Glenview bootlegger, in a photo from World War I. *Jill Ruschli Crane Collection.*

In Philadelphia, the mayor rang the Liberty Bell with a small hammer. Begun's Drugstore in LaCrosse, Wisconsin, handed out free soda pop. At Paramount Studios, Cecil B. DeMille apologized to Gloria Swanson in the middle of a scene: "Excuse me, Miss Swanson. We are going to stop for today....The war is over!"

Chicago rain didn't stop the revelers. From the skyscrapers came a makeshift ticker-tape parade as office workers threw torn-up newspapers and phone books to the streets below. Trolleys, cars and tugboats honked their horns. Air raid sirens blasted out excitement, and church bells all over the city rang out. The saloons were packed by ten o'clock in the morning. Cares and worries were gone forever.

Then came the stark reality; the war was not over. This particular ceasefire was merely ordered to get German diplomats through enemy lines to discuss the end of hostilities. When the secretary of state issued an official denial, the crowds refused to believe it and tore up his message. Chicago's chief of police, John Alcock, ordered one of his policemen to return to work without punishment after the police officer was caught coming out of a bar, half laughing, half crying and cheering. The reason the drunk got off: someone told Alcock the policeman had three sons in France, had just heard they were all well and then heard the war was over.

AND THEY DIDN'T COME BACK 'TIL IT WAS OVER, OVER THERE

Three days later, somebody got the right message, and at 11:00 a.m. on November 11, 1918, the celebrations began anew. Seeing the fake Armistice Day crowds pouring into the bars, a committee of five pastors first appealed to Chicago police chief Alcock to close the saloons. The chief stealthily passed the buck, saying, "It was on the Corporation Council for an opinion on the subject was informed that there was no authority permitting him to close the saloons on such an occasion." Then, the holy men begged the mayor to close the saloons. That didn't work either. Doubt was expressed as to whether the celebrators could have been cleared out anyway. Chicago police reported that a million persons had rampaged, wild with joy and singing patriotic songs, through the Loop.

Every police officer of the two-thousand-member police reserve and a volunteer force of sixteen thousand men was called into service. As many as fifteen policemen were stationed on the most congested downtown corners,

"Chicago receives Armistice News. Streets became scenes of riotous crowds who screamed and shouted until the early morning hours." This photo was taken on the real Armistice Day, November 11, 1918. *Hum Images/Alamy Stock Photo.*

and two or more were placed in every downtown block. For the first time, the reserve police were given full police powers. Victory-mad crowds forgot about law and order in their excitement. By noon, the saloon cash registers were filled to the bursting point. "Mr. Bartender became an essential citizen of first-class." Women flocked into bars, an act that had been unheard of; what's more, they were served. Celebrating citizens flocked to restaurants that were so packed, police manned the doors to keep out all but those with reserved tables. The Chicago Loop "was turned upside down" as crowds everywhere cheered and sang patriotic songs. The proprietors of Berghoff's and Al Tearney's on Clark Street said their employees were entitled to a celebration as much as anyone else.

LANG'S TAVERN[5]

Glenview wasn't any different. A block behind Rugen Stores over by the lumberyard, the old tavern, later called Grandpa's, across from the train station on Prairie Street was constructed in 1898. Leo N. Lang purchased the place in 1902. Location, location, location made Lang's place one of the natural parlors of the patriotic jolly-fest.

As everyone celebrated the first real Armistice Day on November 11, Leo Lang decided to take a ride in his Hupmobile. Who knows, maybe he was on his way to pick up ice. His obituary explained it all:

> *A saloonkeeper met with a very sad accident…while crossing the Chicago, Milwaukee & St. Paul railroad tracks. His machine was struck by the 8:30 fast mail train coming from Chicago. The machine was set afire after being struck. Mr. Lang was also very badly burned. Funeral services were held from his late residence in Glenview. Monday, a.m., interment at St. Henry's cemetery. He leaves to mourn one daughter and other relatives.*

After the ghastly accident, Leo's daughter, Helene, like many dedicated women of those early days, took over the bar business to become one of Glenview's first "whisper sisters."

A few of Leo's friends thought he might have celebrated too much. They also lamented the lack of gates at the train intersection. Back during the

L.N. Lang's, which later became Rugen's Tavern and is now known as Grandpa's Place. *Glenview History Center.*

horse days, only five to ten years earlier, when riders lackadaisically crossed the tracks, the trains were able to slow down and let them pass. With the faster trains, drivers who rode "horsey" time would eventually learn about "train" time. Give it to the good old days, when the guy riding the horse was king of the road.

Another reservation that lingered in the cloud of Lang's death concerned a small article about the Hupp Motor Car Corporation, which advertised that public officials needn't inspect the brakes of their latest model motor cars. Specifically, it was reported, "Once the *steelraulic* brakes…have been adjusted, the owner can forget he has any brakes." Could Leo have forgotten that he had any brakes?

Herb Rugen returned from the Great War in 1919 to his love, Helene, and they married. By the beginning of Prohibition, Lang's place had been renamed Herb Rugen's Soft Drinks. Nothing like hiding in plain sight.

The Rugen family ran the bar for the next fifty years. When Herb died, his daughter Jeanne ran it. For a good many of those years, it was said Rugen's Tavern was a quiet little off-track betting place, and some insiders said it was the most extensive book on the North Shore. Upon remodeling the upstairs rooms, workers found numerous complicated phone lines connecting the little parlor to major racetracks around the country. In 1977, Jeanne Rugen retired, having spent half a century doling out beers to the regulars, and sold it to Tom Dwyer, who renamed it Grandpa's. The latest owner, Kevin Templeton, said it is in honor of his grandfather and in tribute to all grandpas.

THE ANTI-BEERS SNEAK IN

Just before the 1920s, Glenview talk was drunk on the anti-saloon sentiment. The Protestant drys argued that the disgusting saloon owners forced the "demon alcohol" on ignorant immigrants. German settlers, especially those from Wilmette and Glenview, felt especially targeted. They had emigrated from a country whose oldest brewery was built in the year 1040.[6] "That's 26 years before the Norman Conquest of England, 175 years before the Magna Carta, 477 years before Martin Luther's 95 Theses, and 736 years before the Declaration of Independence. The second oldest brewery was founded in 1050." Compare that to the oldest brewery in the United States still in the brewing business, Yuengling's, established in 1829.

These roadhouses, inns and dance halls were good business. Once part and parcel of the old family-owned hostels, catering to the weary long-distance horse or stagecoach travelers, by the early '20s, they welcomed carloads of people from Chicago and the North Shore suburbs. Automobiles were the rage now, and people were looking for reasons and places to drive. These swarms grew as Prohibition wore on, especially in Glenview. The reason for all this success might have had much to do with something called the four-mile limit.

CHAPTER 2

TALK ABOUT YOUR RAW DEALS

Glenview wasn't like the suburbs north along the lake, where Prohibition had been raging bullheaded since the beginning of the century. Evanston, after all, was home to the Woman's Christian Temperance Union and proud of it. Gross Point, a beefy farm town bordering just west of Wilmette, was soon to be eradicated. It was already a flailing little mess, thanks to a pint-sized rule called the four-mile limit, slyly jargoned into a township law by Northwestern University when it was still Garrett College. The school had appropriated the muscle that would keep the North Shore dry for the next 120 years. This is how it came about.[7]

In 1647, Father Marquette literally put Gross Point on the map as he canoed to a skimpy jut of land sticking out into the lake that he named Grosse Pointe. Fur trappers and various traders had a copacetic arrangement with the Native Americans, which gradually disappeared as treaties transpired. During this time, the towns from Rogers Park through Glencoe evolved from the loosely dubbed Grosse Pointe Territory. The spellings evolved as time went on. In 1833, the Treaty of Chicago forced the Potawatomi to give up their five million acres and leave their homes on what would one day become the cultivated North Shore.

One of the first settlers, Edward Mulford, purchased his proverbial swampland for $1.25 an acre, built a tavern/stagecoach stop/post office and houses and called it Ridgevill. (That's how he spelled it—Ridgevill.) In 1850, nine men from Ohio came calling, looking to buy 379 acres with little money and an abundance of zeal. Mulford, proud of his growing town, was happy to oblige. In the Ohioans' quest for a spiritual and moral community, they plugged in a little rule that prohibited a drop of liquor to exist within four miles of their holy boundaries. The Methodists were establishing a highly principled community. Mulford was selling a swamp.

A decade before the Methodist spiritual arrival, German immigrants, escaping the treacheries of their village, Trier, took the little money they saved and placed themselves and their hefty Catholic families on ships in the crowded lower berths with the illness, rats, insects, filth and lack of food. The stench of the incoming vessels was so foul that the people in the harbors could smell the stink a mile before the ships docked. They made their way to the Grosse Pointe Territory, which is now Wilmette, where they purchased the lakeshore property of Antoine Ouilmette. He was married to a Potawatomi woman, and an 1833 treaty motivated the couple to move on to Council Bluff, Iowa, to meet with the rest of her family as they tried to resettle their lives.

The skilled German farmers settled along Ridge Road, turning down the muddy low land by the lake. Families with names like Engels, Schneider, Hoffman and Steffens were under every certainty that their ship had come in, not the other way around. Glad to finally be free of the yoke of repression and fear of land seizures, they set up their butcher shops, bakeries and saloons. They also continued to celebrate their German culture, including their German *bier*. In only ten years, they had constructed St. Joseph's Church, built roads and established the New Trier township. These plucky, hardworking families admirably resurrected their lives from old Trier into the new village of Gross Point.

A mile east, farsighted entrepreneurs purchased land along the lake from the early Germans. Renaming it after its original settlers, anglicized to Wilmette, they advertised appealing house plans in parklike settings. Protestants and Methodists built their churches, attracting families charmed by the opportunity to create a new community based on prosperity and conservative moral values. The new railroad was a plus. So was getting out of the drunken, dirty industrial cities where the immigrants descended worse than the seventeen-year locusts. Contracts were signed. Communities were formed. Townships were established. The four-mile limit stayed put.

During the early 1900s, the towns that evolved from the Grosse Pointe Territory settled into a pattern of rugged efficiency and religious affluency— affluency in a laudable way. Their aims were true, as they emulated the

Left to right: Frank Meier, William Kinge, Bill Rengel, Mike Loutsch and John Loutsch in the Shallick Tavern, Gross Point, 1903. Advertising behind the bar includes "Angauer Bitters," "Paul Pohl's Weiss Beer" and "Pepsin Calisara Bitters." Ed Zeutchel owned the saloon at one time. *Courtesy Charles L. Richardson, photographer/Wilmette Historical Museum.*

concepts of the Methodist preachers from Ohio. The dwindling Grosse Point Territory watched the little religious college grow into Northwestern University, the kickoff of the mighty Big Ten.

All this development happened as the Gross Point Germans were still butchering, baking, plowing and brewing. Ridge Road was home to fifteen saloons, the vital source of the town's revenue. Each saloon provided $500 a year to the village of Gross Point, a remarkable amount of proceeds for a town of fewer than one thousand people.

Meanwhile, the temperance movement[8] was rushing in like a spring flood. Temperance originally meant a reduction in the use of alcoholic beverages before it got all mucked up and jampacked with moral, religious and political details. Methodists, Baptists and Congregationalists were all firm in their disapproval of the alcoholic drink. Episcopalian Protestants and German Lutherans were more amenable to the reduction idea. The Lutherans like to say they drank in public and prayed in private, while the other Protestants prayed in public and drank in private. For hundreds of years, maybe thousands, there was a drive to persuade the overindulged to just please quit—or at least cut down. Not to overindulge (sorry) the reader with the ancient history of the Egyptians and Greeks, early America's drys begged discipline about drinking.

Dr. Benjamin Rush, a signer of the Declaration of Independence, warned about overindulgence when describing a dozen health-related issues to his fellow colonists. "Yeah, sure," was the attitude of most of the bigwigs, especially since he knew a drunk who happened "to belch near an open flame and was 'suddenly destroyed.'" Benjamin Franklin wrote an early guide to winemaking and a list of thirteen guiding principles, the first of which was temperance. It is claimed he said, "Beer is proof God loves us." George Washington's dinner ritual included three to four glasses of Madeira wine. As a general, he made it clear that soldiers should continue receiving their daily four ounces of whiskey, saying, "The benefits of arising from moderate use of strong Liquor have been experienced in all Armies and are not to be disputed."

John Adams's morning routine included swigs from his jug of hard cider along with his breakfast of poached salmon with egg sauce, toast with apple butter, ham steak and hash browns. Thomas Jefferson cultivated rye whiskey from his estate's harvest. Despite his wine collection of twenty thousand bottles, the moderate drinker limited himself to three glasses of wine after dinner. James Madison also controlled his intake of alcohol, with the worry that "if you drink too much, it will make you hop around like a cork," describing a cork exploding from a champagne bottle. His wife, Dolley, was the hostess of happy hours in early Washington, D.C., when she provided an open invitation to the local legislators. Children had daily

An August 1, 1831 poster. Believing alcohol would prevent cholera, the woman's child is given brandy, while the other players appear to have reached their limit. Even in the 1920s, doctors prescribed a small of amount of whiskey to children suffering from "la grippe" (flu) or "pharyngitis" (sore throat). *Courtesy National Library of Medicine. Artist, Robert Seymour.*

snorts in those days to protect them from ravages of diseases like cholera and were routinely given shots of whiskey to cure everyday ailments like la grippe (the flu) and pharyngitis (sore throat).

Temperance movements had already been blazing in Ohio[9] in the 1830s. The rise in industrialization led the fundamental religious to feel God would no longer bless the United States. Women asked their husbands how they were supposed to raise upstanding children if their men were coming home tipsy or, worse, drunk. At the same time, the Pabst, Schlitz and Anheuser-Busch businesses flourished due to improved manufacturing practices and a thriving railroad system that delivered their beer quickly. It also helped that the beer manufacturers had no problem paying the saloons' license fees, which could be up to a whopping $1,500.

"The Overshadowing Curse—The Legalized Saloon," an Anti-Saloon League poster, circa 1917. *Photo by American Issue Publishing Co., courtesy Library of Congress.*

Ultra-conservative Maine passed a prohibition law in 1851, smug in its belief that its local laws would stop the flow of the wicked drink. What it got was a lack of enforcement. Hotels, restaurants and drinking establishments maneuvered a little strategy called the Bangor Plan. Twice a year, the drinking establishments went to court to pay a set fine for the said sale of alcoholic beverages. In between the court dates, the police simply looked the other way. In 1855, Irish working-class rioters stormed the Portland City Hall upon learning their teetotaling mayor was storing $1,600 worth of liquor. The law was repealed a year later.

Dr. John Kennicott,[10] who arrived in Glenview in 1836, was the postmaster when most postmasters were also bartenders to the stagecoach trade. Dr. William Kennicott, his brother, became Chicago's first dentist, and his office was located at the Eagle Tavern. A diary page of his neighbor, August Conant, noted on January 11, 1837, that he had a "temperance meeting at his house, and a society was formed." Temperance organizations were strong in the early 1800s and obviously in Glenview, as well.

Religious doctrines, locked into a moral vision, truly believed the unsanctified would lead their families to sinful ruin. It was a scary time for these self-blessed people. The torrent of unskilled immigrants who could find work in factories, lived in crowded cities and gathered in the evil saloons profoundly frightened the more traditional families. So, they moved to the suburbs, escaping the filthy saloons, immigrants, dust and grit of corruption. They used every opportunity to apply their strong ethics, firm discipline and fine principles in their new villages, deftly building welcoming towns along the North Shore. What was not appreciated was that all-male saloons provided the tired, lonely worker a place to get news, make friends, receive mail, have a meal and, of course, drink—many times to excess. Temperance crusaders were able to convince their followers that one drop of the evil drink would not only kill a man but also smite his whole family.

FRANCES WILLARD

In the mid-1800s, Woman's Christian Temperance Unions thrived all over the East and Midwest. Its most passionate cheerleader was Evanston's Frances Willard,[11] called Frank by her friends. With the help of her live-in secretary, Anna Adams Gordon, she lobbied, petitioned, lectured and wrote hundreds of publications. It wasn't unusual for her to travel over thirty thousand miles in a year, educating her public in over four hundred speaking lectures. Her educating entailed a "Home Protection" movement, in which she told women to realize they were not the "weaker" sex. Frances Willard was rampant in her stand against the devastation caused by the legalized drinking traffic. She needed to save women from drinking husbands who beat them and their children after wasting their paychecks in saloons.

This little trace of the gentle sex supported suffrage and prohibition. She championed daycare for working women, succeeded in raising the age of consent and passed labor reforms such as the eight-hour workday. She also established medical dispensaries, kindergartens, Sunday schools, lodging houses and low-price restaurants. As president of the Woman's Christian Temperance Union, she was influential in passing not only the Volstead Act but also women's right to vote. Even though she died in 1898, her strength was powerful. Willard's respect for the achievement of women was paramount in advancing the lives of every woman, even if they had never heard of her.

Empowered by the effort of Frances Willard, ladies united in their quest for a more moral community. These tough women's temperance crusaders attacked the saloons with hymn singing and organized marches through

Left: Frances Elizabeth Caroline "Frank" Willard, first dean of women at Northwestern University, longtime president of the Woman's Christian Temperance Union, founder of the World Woman's Christian Temperance Union and first president of the National Council of Women of the United States. *Courtesy Library of Congress (unknown photograph, restored by Adam Cuerden).*

Right: Carry A. Nation on her way to a hatchetation. *Courtesy John L. Binder and Getty Images.*

the streets—mainly the saloon-littered streets. These beautiful women sat themselves right at the source of the demons, the grimy, putrid, nasty taverns. Dropping to their knees in fitful pleading, they demanded that the tavern be closed. One town's crafty response to the ladies' demonstrations was to pass laws against their marches. The unweak and untimid women pressed on. These proud cheerleaders' mighty aim was to help their poor immigrant neighbors.

In 1900, a hog jaw of a woman, Carry A. Nation[12]—as in "carry a nation"—and her committed followers smashed bars in Kansas. Proud of her thirty-two arrest records for her "hatchetations," this six-foot-tall cheerleader for the drys also educated her hymn-singing followers about the harmful effect of tight corsets on women's vital organs.

The temperance movement had become full-blown.

WAYNE WHEELER AND HIS WHEELER-DEALER
ANTI-SALOON LEAGUE

Temperance was discussed, argued and ranted everywhere, especially in saloons. It polarized the relationships of family, friends and neighbors. When the political arena was injected with this kind of antagonism, calm discussion went out the window. Using this energy, a shrewd Ohio lawyer became the kingpin of the Anti-Saloon League (ASL), growing it into a national organization that was the first to use pressure politics around a single issue. Wayne Wheeler's[13] single-mission, bipartisan propaganda machine led to the national outlaw of all alcohol manufacture, sale and delivery. The Anti-Saloon League, in a very exacting strategy, set out to save America from itself. The ASL and its gladrag gang of drys set upon the hungover American public like the offense team in a T formation, forcing their standards of life on a smaller, less inclined number of people. That minority, as extensive as it was repressed, thought of drinking as perfectly innocent. For them, it was cultural, not habitual. Irish, German and Italian Catholics brought their drinking culture as they immigrated, as did Jews and German Lutherans. Drinking was no more unholy than the Bible. On the other hand, Wayne Wheeler hated liquor more than he hated the devil. He was just a kid when he watched in horror as a drunk farmhand stabbed himself in the leg with a pitchfork. "Drink will never touch my lips," swore young Wayne.

Wayne Bidwell Wheeler, leader of the Anti-Saloon League and the master of propaganda. *Courtesy Library of Congress.*

The law school scholar from Oberlin was so chained to the power of temperance that he bought himself a bicycle and pedaled his way to towns beyond his college, lecturing about the evils of liquor. His God-given gift of gab, along with the adulation of his passioned crowds, fastballed him to a long stretch in Washington, D.C. He brainwashed the masses on the evils of booze with overblown stories of the wallowing drunks passed out in gutters while their families suffered the depravity of the streets. That's when he knew he could sell an igloo to an Eskimo. The biggest buyers of his "Wheelerisms" were the gaslighted puppets in the dry states. Wheeler's indoctrination was remarkable in that it worked so well and so fast. "The saloons must go" was one of his favorite sayings.

Wheeler used wedge politics, which conducts an either-or approach, forcing the person to take a side. Do you love school, or do you love being stupid? The question became, do you love being a drunk weasel, or do you love your family? Ruthless in his method of activism, he was most effective in rural areas, where he concentrated on how legislators voted. He used emotion based on patriotism to cleverly persuade those running for office with threats to withdraw campaign endorsements and, worse, money. He had no problem revealing embarrassing information to make local politicians vote for dry laws. Using the same tactics, he pressured local police to arrest saloon owners and take their licenses if they violated closing hours or served women and minors, and he provided witnesses to seal the deal. He crisscrossed the country, inspiring needed constituents through churches, town halls and the media. He mobilized these same organizations to fear the growing number of immigrants pouring into cities. Fear became the predicator, mover and result. Wayne Wheeler expressed his measures succinctly:

> I'll do it the way the bosses do it: with minorities. We'll vote against all the men in office who won't support our bills. We'll vote for candidates who will promise to. We are teaching these crooks that breaking their promises to us is surer of punishment than going back on their bosses, and some day they will learn that all over the United States—and we'll have national Prohibition.

Not so fast, was the response. One (among many) letter writer to the *Chicago Tribune* complained, "It is high time somebody was speaking out against the fanatics....Congress is still too frightened to vote its own convictions."

The ASL-owned American Issue Publishing House produced forty tons of mail per month. In the Chicago area, Wheeler worked tirelessly, pushing for a local option referendum. It was passed in 1907, and by 1910, 40 of 102 Illinois counties and 1,059 of the state's townships and precincts had turned dry. It was incredibly successful in the Protestant areas. Even though more than half of the U.S. population believed in the right to drink, local option referendums prevailed. The immigrants were screwed. They had no way out.[14]

That was the circumstance with the Germans of Gross Point. Things just were not sitting quite right as they viewed their neighbors to the east. The attitudes of the growing temperance movement were gaining traction in the clubs and churches of the Protestant persuasions. A strong affiliation of Wilmette and Winnetka women was determined to "save" what in their minds were graceless German immigrants who thrived in Gross Point. It's not that they didn't like filthy, drunk, ignorant immigrants. It's just that, in their opinions, the Gross Pointers were filthy, drunk and ignorant. Their thinking was, subtract the drunk part, clean them up, educate them and, voila, the Germans would turn into good Americans, just like them. It was evident to the drys; the immigrant's task was to fit in, and step number one was closing the saloons. To be sure, if every saloon in America was shuttered, the foreigners could be Americans. In her thrust to aid the Gross Pointers and, more importantly, the North Shore, no one hustled it up better than Gertrude M. Thurston. Since women could not vote yet, the fiery crusader urged her fellow members of the Winnetka Women's Club to support the dry movement by "using our influence and our tongues in reminding our husbands to vote." Media influence, in respect to society's timidity, wasn't about to proclaim what infliction she envisioned for their men if they did not vote dry.

THE FOUR-MILE LIMIT

The group, among others, sprang upon the people of Gross Point in an all-out war. In Wilmette, the four-mile limit became the battle cry, and the battlefield became the fifteen bars along Ridge Road. The crusaders singing their hymns with ultra-intensity proposed to stomp out the saloons. They avoided the hatchetations of one of their mentors, instead setting up a robust schedule of sitting outside the bars (even in the winter—especially in the winter) and pushing themselves into the intolerable dens of filth, spittle, urine, spilled beer, profanity and even the shame of the well-bosomed naked tart painting that adorned most bars. They implored saloon owners to quit their trade for the benefit of the wives and children of the drunken…well… drunks. They had a point worth considering.

Some men had their shot and a beer. Others really did stumble home drunk or, worse, freeze to death in the snow. Whole paychecks disappeared into the cash registers of saloon owners. Not that the saloon owners minded, no matter how friendly they were. Thanks to cheerleaders Frances Willard, Carry A. Nation and Gertrude M. Thurston, the housewives could finally put their feet down. What the crusaders didn't understand, or just didn't care about, was that the German families who lived along Ridge Road weren't immigrants. They had founded and developed Gross Point long before the reformers moved in.

Above: Glenview School, closed for the flu/pneumonia/diphtheria epidemic as Prohibition roared into Glenview. *From Glenview, the First Centennial.*

Left: These posters dotted Glenview windows during the 1920 flu/pneumonia/diphtheria epidemic. *Jill Ruschli Crane Collection.*

Chicago's finance committee asserted that the situation was "far from alarming," foreshadowing how the city fathers would handle the thorny issues of Prohibition.

Edwin Meltzer, the Glenview health officer, closed the Glenview School. The Cramer and Haupt families were quarantined with red "keep out" posters in their windows. The epidemic had reached its peak by the end of February, declining to claim any Glenview lives, except for Mr. and Mrs. Clavey, whose son and daughter-in-law, recent residents of Glencoe, both died of the flu, making their precious grandbaby an orphan. Glenview mourned.

The epidemic didn't stop the city fathers from scheduling village improvements. Bids were in for cement sidewalks on Shermer Avenue, public hearings were posted on sewer proposals and plans were made to widen Milwaukee Avenue.

Glenview's three policemen[17] continued their regular duties, one of the most important being watching for speeders at the Death Curve on Waukegan Road. It was big news when a new officer went on duty and immediately arrested a speeder, telling Judge Cole, "He took the curve on high, Your Honor." The prisoner reasoned, "I always do things fast." His Honor retorted, "See how fast you can dig up fifteen dollars and costs."

Three years later, on June 8, 1924, broke and broken Gross Point was annexed into Wilmette. Sadness and defeat consumed the ex-town. The *Daily Herald* reported:

> *A bride weeps beery tears as dry Wilmette annexes "free and easy" Gross Point. The previous night, the few taverns still alive did a record business. Even moderate drinkers found it exciting, but the crowds could only sing sad songs despite the drunken sparkle.*
>
> *The next morning, mourning brought scenes of the town funeral. Black crepe hung over the few taverns. One saloon owner left a single glass of booze on one of his barstools. If the drys had expected raids on these evil dens, they were disappointed. The Wilmette police chief had warned the tavern owners of the need to obey the law to the letter of the law. The saloon owners, thankful that, for the most part, he overlooked their previous few years of booze hawking, closed their joints at midnight on the sorrowful day. Ironically, there were several raids in Glenview, but on Sunday morning, the booze was back on the bar and drinkers on the barstools.*

In old dearly departed Gross Point, a man mollified the others, "Cheer up, Pal, there's Glenview in the distance, within walking distance, if one can't wait for the bus. Folks over in Glenview have never heard of Volstead."

CHAPTER 3

WHAT PROHIBITION?[18]

B eer was downed. Drinks were served. Cocktails were invented to hide the taste of the bad booze. Local roadhouses sprouted like tulips in springtime. Looking to escape the grime, dirt and scum, Chicagoans hopped on trains to Shermerville[19] to drink in the neighborhood bars and pass out in their lovely parks. It wasn't pretty. The city fathers renamed the town Northbrook in hopes of dodging its reputation as a drinking town. Perhaps the only reason Glenview avoided this little snare was because the Waukegan Road saloons were too far away for the inebriated to stagger back to the station. By the end of Prohibition, there were over five hundred bars, saloons, resorts, speakeasies, blind pigs and nightclubs along Waukegan Road from Chicago's north boundary to Lake Cook Road. They screeched to a halt at Wilmette's dry border.

Everyone wanted a pop—farmers, thirsty Germans, wealthy couples from Winnetka and Northwestern college kids. Even young socialites were coming into the bars. It was the new hobby. Henry Zeutchel, son of a Gross Point saloon owner, opened the River Inn on Wagner Road, which posed as a skeet-shooting gun club. The original roadhouses, John Dilg's Inn and Haut's Place, were faring well due to the taverns' yearly licensing fees. During the dry era, licenses[20] to supposedly illegal bars could cost up to $1,000 a year. "In surrounding Cook County, the sheriff was paid to look the other way in the unincorporated areas, as were the police in many of the individual suburbs....For years, the position of Cook County Sheriff...was an opportunity for the office holder to become rich."[21]

WITH COMPLIMENTS FROM

THE RIVER INN

GUN CLUB
TRAPSHOOTING

H. Zeutchel

Lake Avenue and Wagner Road

Left: Henry Zeutchel, son of Gross Point Saloon owner Ed Zeutchel, opened the River Inn as a gun club. *From the* Daily Herald, *November 2, 1923.*

Below: Folks in a saloon. Looking at the background, it appears there was no shortage of bottled booze. *Courtesy imageBroker/Alamy Stock Photo.*

Like they did before Prohibition, men still hung out in the Glenview saloons, playing cards, talking farming and automobiles and complaining about kids' lack of morals. In 1920, they were relieved when Glenview passed a law prohibiting improper and immoral dancing.[22] They drank illegal beer and pondered how this Prohibition thing even happened, gloating that the township had defeated the anti-saloons by 870 to 359.[23] Too bad the rest of the nation didn't agree. Prohibition was here to stay. The early reviews were mixed.

PROHIBITION—A JOKE

On January 22, 1920, two letters to the editor in the *Chicago Tribune* stood out. One writer complained, "The *Tribune* appears to enjoy printing letters coming from 'whiskey friends' who are put out because of the Prohibition law.…Like it or not, Prohibition will close most of the jails." On the other side, "Many American citizens of good standing are taking Prohibition for what it is—a joke."[24]

The Chicago grape juice company president[25] on Sedgwick Street was charged with selling grape juice with 7.87 percent alcohol after five schoolboys were found drunk. He was one of the 34,343 arrests in Chicago in 1920, which was pretty low compared to 1918, when the police arrested 110,819 people with a smaller police department and no Volstead Act.

The government dealt a low blow[26] to the toe-the-line saloon owners who decided the law was the law and turned their bars into ice cream parlors. When liquor was legal, the owners paid $6.60 a gallon in taxes. It was the price of doing business. But those saloons that paid taxes in advance were stunned when the government wouldn't credit their paid taxes back to them.

Fabian Franklin,[27] Johns Hopkins University doctorate mathematician turned journalist, wrote a hefty portrayal insisting that Prohibition was overwhelmingly unconstitutional in its regulations on personal habits. He argued the job of the Constitution was to preserve the fundamentals. Furthermore, it was supposed to protect minorities like the working class,

Agents from the Prohibition Bureau with a captured still. They may have been proud of themselves, but Chicago law enforcement thwarted their penalty efforts. *Courtesy Science History Images/Alamy Stock Photo.*

immigrants, Catholics, Lutherans and Jews. That meant the average American citizen who wanted a drink had three choices: A. submit to the law, B. nullify the Constitution, C. break the law. It is not surprising that a good many citizens regarded the last choice as the best. Fabian Franklin went on to say, "The great guilt is not that of the law-breakers, but that of the lawmakers." In the end, the Volstead Act led to over-aggressive invasions of privacy and unwarranted searches. A worse result was the sheer arrogance in the newborn disrespect of the law.

To enforce the law in the Midwest, Major A.V. Dalrymple, Captain Hubert Howard and 250 agents were appointed to crack down on the newly classified criminals as representatives of what was officially known as the Federal Prohibition Bureau. The Central Department territory included Illinois, Indiana, Michigan and Wisconsin. In just ten months, they had exposed illegal traffic, confiscated $4,000 of bootlegger booze, destroyed 2,500 stills and reported 1,840 cases of liquor law violations to Chicago's district attorney. But nobody went to jail. The problem? A whole host of pivotal Chicago people—federal judges, U.S. commissioners and district attorneys—blocked their efforts. They couldn't produce warrants. The police wouldn't arrest. It was only 1920, and already bribe money was

Immoral dancing in the 1920s. *Sueddeutsche Zeitung Photo/Alamy Stock Photo.*

working. Besides that, Chicago was a drinking town for workers like the cops. Dalrymple appealed to the Washington, D.C. bigshots for more agents. He only got ten. A month later, he resigned.[28] Captain Howard, who had fled the agency a month earlier, said he could have made a million dollars in bribes. They didn't have a clue about the workingmen's culture like Al Capone and the North Side gangs did. In terms of incoming crime, things were just warming up.

Glenview presented a far calmer situation. Farmland was interspersed with friends and family who had grown up and known each other for generations, who lived in a culture that worked hard and lived for the common good. Drinking a good bier now and then was no crime, especially if it was homemade. Few didn't get their work done, especially since there was so much work to do. As mentioned earlier, roadhouses and inns dotted the downtown, as did a couple of dance halls. The dance halls were mainly open on the weekends and holidays, necessitating Glenview lawmakers to pass that ordinance about immoral dancing in 1920. The lawmakers didn't even think about drinking issues.

THE GLENVIEW BANK ROBBERY[29]

What the thriving little town really needed was a bank. Businesses and farms were growing like weeds, and while handshakes might still be trustworthy, they were hardly practical. Citizens had been taking their cash to the Rugen Stores to keep money in their store safe for security. Charles Rugen and a few Glenview citizens came to the rescue, and with an investment of $30,000, the Glenview State Bank was officially founded. Charles Rugen worked part time with a telephone, a borrowed clock, a typewriter and a hand-operated adding machine, keeping track of his customers' money and lending it out for a small fee. Like all the Rugens, his priority was being of service to his town.

Within a year, the money business turned out to be so good that Charles and his businessmen friends built a bank next to John Dilg's Glen View Inn and opened on May 17, 1921. At the grand opening, the newly formed Glenview Civic Association celebrated with a dinner dance at the Blue Heron just east of the river on Glenview Road. The group's purpose was to provide Glenview with social recreations through athletics, plays and other amusements. It ran the yearly Community Day, which turned into a three-day fundraising carnival called Glenview Days in future years.

Glenview State Bank. Notice the Glenview Bear Fountain in its original location. *From Glenview, the First Centennial.*

Charles Rugen invited the public to visit the new bank any time between 9:00 a.m. and 9:00 p.m. Transactions were hand posted by the one newly hired full-time cashier, Fred J. Christensen. The young teller had impressive credentials, having worked for six years at Drexel State Bank in Chicago. He had recently moved to Glenview to a home close to the bank with his wife and three-year-old daughter.

Fred loved his job, and Glenview loved Fred. The locals liked putting their money where they could talk to such an easygoing man with a pleasant, helpful way about him. When parents brought their children, they discovered Christensen would coax the kiddos to open their own small savings accounts so they could watch their pennies grow as opposed to spending it on useless candy, which would only bring on cavities and pain in the dentist chair. Glenview was so proud of this twenty-four-year-old man. When he hired this man, Charles Rugen did one of his best day's work.

Saturday morning was cool on September 24, 1921. Fred Christensen walked to the bank with his three-year-old, who dilly-dallied among the neighbors' gardens, while he thought how good it had been chewing the fat with his dad on his front porch the night before. His dad had come into town from Fred's hometown of St. John, Indiana, with all the neighborhood gossip. In turn, Fred's dad was glad to see how well Fred and his little family had settled into this friendly little community named Glenview. When they neared the railroad crossing, the little girl and her daddy chitchatted with the flagman, F.C. Clavey. Once Fred arrived at the bank, he sent the tot rambling home.

About 8:30 a.m., R.S. Mandel, who was moseying along Glenview Road, passing the new bank, thought he might have heard gunshots, but the noise could have been falling tiles in a drainage area where the new sewer was being laid. Curious, he peered through the glass of the bank door. All he saw was the nightlight burning, so he assumed the noise was, indeed, breaking tiles and resumed his morning constitutional. At about this same time, Police Chief Schultz noticed a Ford Touring car in front of the bank.

"Cashier's Mysterious Murder," a photo diagram of the police theory of the murder. *From* Chicago Tribune, *copyright 1921, under license.*

After Mandel passed the bank, John Dilg, owner of the Glen View Inn, happened to follow him to make a deposit. He opened the front door and observed the vault's main door standing wide open, yet the inner doors to the cash compartment were locked. Suspicious, Dilg called out to Christensen. No answer. Dilg took another step toward the grating that separated the inner offices, and there on the floor was his new friend, Fred, blood flowing from his chest and his .22-caliber gun still in his right hand. Dilg called Chief of Police Ernest Schultz, who hurried to the bank with a doctor. The cashier had been shot in his left side under his arm, leaving a gaping hole and a .38-caliber bullet.

Fred Christensen had put up a brave battle for his bank. The trigger of his pistol had been pulled. The hammer indented the cartridge but failed to explode. The nervy clerk had evidently seen the robber and made the brave move that cost him his life. Two shots were fired by the murderer, one piercing the heart and lung of his victim, the other entering an office partition. Confronted with the foul deed, the assassin made the wise decision not to rifle the vault and escaped through a basement window, which was found jimmied open. David Lindstrom, photographer for Captain Williams A. Evans's bureau of identification, took pictures of nine perfect fingerprints, which were described as the "best clews [*sic*] in the world." There were no witnesses to the comings or goings of the murderers, but it's possible the Ford Touring car was the getaway car.

It was not until the coroner's physician, Dr. Rinehardt, made the examination that the public was informed of the murder. The report had gone out that the young Fred had succumbed to a heart attack. It wasn't until late in the day that Mrs. Christensen was told that her husband was the victim of a bandit's gun, not a heart attack. The inventory of the vault's contents showed that nothing had been disturbed. Chicago police were on the lookout for the murderer/robber. Glenview was aroused at the enormity of the crime, and both Charlie Rugen and Chief Ernie Schultz would spare no effort to hunt down the murderer and bring him to justice. They offered a reward of $1,000.

The news appeared in the September 26, 1921 *Chicago Daily Tribune*:

> *Investigation into the death of Fred Christensen, cashier of the Glen View State Bank who was found dead Saturday, a bullet wound through his side, on the floor of the bank, showed that more than one man participated in the shooting and attempted robbery....Chief Schultz indicated that he had received some vital information and expected to have the men in custody before the week was over.*

A few days later, the chief reported that the murder was the work of a local amateur criminal. He further said that to find the culprit, he required everyone in Glenview to have their fingerprints taken. He went on to say that authorities were already watching one resident. Authorities did a lot of crime watching in those days. This was one of three early violent murders in Glenview that were never held accountable.

CARD OF THANKS
I wish to extend my sincere thanks to the people of Glenview for their very great kindness and sympathy shown towards me in the late bereavement of my dear husband, Fred.
Mrs. Fred J. Christman.

"A Note of Thanks" from Fred Christensen's wife. *From* Daily Herald *(Chicago), October 28, 1921.*

A month later, a little blurb in the local papers welcomed the family of John A. Meyers as cashier of Glenview State Bank. They took their residence in the Weber home in Glenview.

More than a decade later, it would be seen that Fred Christensen wasn't the only hero at the Glenview State Bank.

BEER WARS IN THE BIG CITY[30]

In Chicago's city streets, the gangsters hijacked each other's trucks, robbed breweries, hustled drugstore owners and bribed cops to look away from their substantial moneymaking schemes. Policemen observed it was better to be bribed than shot. Then, too, a little extra coin always came in handy. From the city's first days, "early gangs were thugs in the employ of the political machines, intimidating opposition candidates and funneling votes to the boss. In return, the politicians and police chiefs would turn a blind eye to illegal gambling and prostitution rings."

Then came Prohibition.

At first, the small gangs used the knock-'em-down, shoot-'em-up theory to protect their breweries and speakeasies. As the illegal money came pouring in, it was time to get smart. The intelligent guys like John Torrio,[31] Al Capone's mentor, hired lawyers to keep the arrested out of jail. Millions of dollars needed to be laundered, which led to the hiring of accountants. Shipping logistics required careful planning. While the thugs concentrated on their grudges and artillery, the savvy gangsters slowly became businessmen. It became apparent that success rested on cooperation between gangs, which eventually became the syndicate.

OLD FRIENDS ARE KINDLY BOOTLEGGERS[32]

Far enough from Chicago's maddening gangs, the roadhouses at Glenview and Waukegan Roads had socked away some booze during the year leading up to Prohibition. Citizens may not have liked the new law, but they obeyed it since it was the law. There was an assumption that people would not be expecting to drink. It was Prohibition, after all. Yet when the saved booze ran out, thirsty citizens looked to the waiter/bootlegger for supplies without any repercussions. In Glenview, the three law enforcement officials quickly looked the other way. The bootleggers and barkeeps were their neighbors, and all they were doing was delivering what merely happened to be barrels of beer to the local roadhouses. In one saloon, "a motorcycle roared up, and a policeman came in and rather hurriedly drank two glasses of wine. He talked with the bartender, and a few customers then left by a side entrance. He was no more noticed by management or patrons than any other customer."

There were all sorts of bootleggers.[33] The term *bootlegger* comes from the Civil War, when soldiers carried illicit liquor in their boots to sneak it into their camps. A bootlegger could be the director of a giant organization, like Al Capone, or a pharmacist in a drugstore, planted and/or paid by gangsters, or not. All he had to do was fill medical prescriptions for whiskey, gin or beer to treat a toothache or the flu, the patient being limited to only a pint every ten days. Amazingly, Walgreens, the drugstore proud of its 20 Chicagoland locations in 1919, grew another 480 of its famous corner stores by 1929. Of course, medical alcohol probably had nothing to do with its growth, as explained by an ad where Walgreens explained its newfound profits by having raised the price of its "Walgreen Double Rich Malted Milk" from fifteen to twenty cents.

Then, too, there were the almost silent bootleggers; yes, the reverends and rabbis with locks on all that sacramental wine, perhaps tempted by charming but unscrupulous players offering new pews, stained-glass windows and fresh frocks for the altar boys. Another type of bootlegger, mainly from the wine regions of California, honestly sold wine bricks—ahem, homemade grape juice packages—for $2 with a stern warning "against dissolving the brick in a gallon of water, adding sugar shaking daily and decanting after three weeks." Just before Prohibition, these grape concentrates cost $9.50 a ton. By 1924, each ton was $375. It's no wonder Cesare Mondavi gave up his tiny grocery store in Minnesota for the good life in California.

The overworked housewife was another type of bootlegger. A whole new cottage industry sprang up, increasing the family budget by producing bathtub gin, so called because the bottles didn't fit under the short kitchen spigots, and the entrepreneurs had to resort to their bathtub faucets. Mobsters furnished the corn, sugar and yeast and then bought the "stuff" from the families at fifty to seventy-five cents a gallon and sold it to the speakeasies for six dollars. There hasn't been an ounce of research to confirm that any housewife or houseman in Glenview ever succumbed to the use of bathtubs for bottling—basement washtubs, maybe.

More common was the broke son of a gun with a truck who climbed on the bandwagon or, more aptly, the booze wagon. Young Ed Kelly was well groomed for his position. Before arriving in Glenview, Ed grew up helping his dad run the family roadhouse. The elder Ed Kelly[34] had spent years on the South Side of Chicago as a saloon owner and manager of the Artesians, a semipro baseball team. Maybe it's a myth, or perhaps most semipro teams owned saloons on their team play lots, but he pitched and, in his off innings, ran back to his bar to siphon beer for the batters. The early days of South Side baseball got him in touch with Charles Comiskey. He was a trophied bowler, and he was also your typical Irish cop, buddying up with politicians

from Gross Point, with a good idea and plenty of German and Lithuanian support, making it happen. In the '20s, local Glenview saloon owners had it made with their old friend from Wilmette, who kept them plied with quality beer. The gangs hadn't discovered Glenview. Yet…

THE GROSS POINT BOOTLEGGER[37]

The South Side had the Capone gang. The North Side had the Bugs Moran gang. Des Plaines had the Roger Touhy gang. Glenview had Matt Hoffman, and he had no gang. Hoffman was born in 1898, second of six kids to Luxembourg immigrants Peter and Catherine Hoffman, who owned a truck farm on Old Glenview Road near many of the original Trier settlers, including the Schneider family. The farmers were up by five o'clock in the morning, coaxing their crops, tending to relentless weeds, dependent on the weather; one year too much rain, the next too little. Always working, planting, worrying, seeding, hoeing, worrying, weeding, worrying, picking, harvesting, worrying, hoping to sell a few cucumbers and tomatoes to the Wilmette elite. It was a tough life, much like the dozens of generations before them. With their six children, Peter and Kate unobtrusively built up their little truck farm.

Matt wasn't born a beer peddler, but he had a tenacious quality that put him on top of the world, unfortunately leading to his heartrending downfall. Matt's other overriding quality was that of a protector. This all started before he was even a teenager. Something not uncommon in Wilmette, much less life, is when one clique decides to demonstrate their swagger over the weak. Such was the case in 1907, when a group of four east side bullies beat up Hoffman's friend little Charlie Bohn. In its aftermath, the bloodied youngster, who had been cleaned up, sewed up and shut up, when questioned by parents, police, doctors and the revered pastor of St. Joe's, Father Netstreater, kept his mouth closed as tight as the twenty stitches in his head.

Charlie Bohn's protector kept his eye on the east side bullies, despite little talks with Father Netstreater and little check-ins between the pastor and Matt's father. Confident of his own thinking, Matt wasn't going to be so stupid as to say one word to the respected pontiff. The English-speaking St. Francis school in eastern Wilmette expanded, transferring Charlie's smart alecks to the newer school. The developing game of football prompted the area schools to arrange healthy competitions for the boys. Matt threw himself into the game, turning his body into a human tank. When game day arrived, Matt seized his opportunity for revenge. Under the guise of good clean fun, he rammed and punched those punks every chance he got.

> *He bore down on the boy opposite him playing left tackle.…He pummeled his opponent play after play, always in the side, against the ribs, and sometimes he shoved an elbow right under his arm. Matt kept this up for three quarters before going at him with a real vengeance in the fourth quarter. He didn't want to be taken out of the game before he had a chance to inflict serious pain on him. Once the fourth quarter started, Matt kept going at his ribs, over and over. Finally, with one minute to go, Matt jammed his left elbow into the boy's side so hard, he heard his bones crack.*[38]

And the east side sissies couldn't do a thing about it. St. Joe won all six games that season.

Toward the end of his adolescence, when baseball was a rural passion, Matt played in Gross Point with the Schneider brothers galore while their sweet sisters took over the stands, cheering. They liked it so much they even played when there wasn't another team, and that's when this story takes place. Paul Schneider, a future cousin-in-law of Matt's, was warming up his pitch on the mound. Maybe they had a few beers before the game, or maybe Paul Schneider was no Hippo Vaughn, but he threw a two-seam fastball and watched in horror as it beaned right on Matt's head. Then, like a bad tennis game, the ball bounced off and turned into a fly ball. The friends, Schneider sisters and brothers watching the game gasped, expecting to rush the charming batter to the hospital. But the guy was still standing, laughing and pointing to his head. Feeling like the joke was on them, Matt explained that when he was kicked in the head by a horse, surgeons had to put a metal plate in his head. The ball bounced because of the safe cushion of hardware buried between Matt's scalp and his gray matter. Matt always was a good time.

Despite the metal plate in his head, he and his childhood sweetheart, tiny winsome neighbor Anna Schneider, full of brothers, fell fully in love. Soon Matt's eventual partners, the bridesmaids and groomsmen celebrated their elegant wedding. In the beginning, he supported her with his job at the North Shore Ice Company, where he had been delivering ice since he was still a teenager, but to be honest, he wanted out.

A little less than a year after their wedding, child number one came along on February 29, 1920. Feeling like the baby's leap year day of birth was a sign

Matt Hoffman (*far right*) during his iceman days, hoisting a block of ice. The three men on the left are unidentified. A few years later, this strength came in handy for transporting half barrels of beer. *Courtesy George R. Pinkowski Jr.*

of good luck, bored with the ice business and intelligent enough to realize Kelvinator's refrigerators were shriveling the ice market, Matt concluded his interaction with the frozen emporiums. He was going to make his mark, smugly realizing the only ice he'd be doling out would be in cocktail glasses. A pretty, young wife and a child called for a Roaring Twenties high-hat. Matt Hoffman was that guy. The iceman go-eth.

THE CURVE

Matt opened a bar in his garage called the Curve, creatively named for the curve in the road in front of his house. He supplied his blind pig with the brew he manufactured behind his house in a weedy drainage ditch between present-day New and Old Glenview Roads. Maybe the weeds were poison ivy or too damp, but certainly not too secret. Ann's brothers used to go trapping along the drainage ditch and came across the open-air brewery as if they had run into Sears Tower. Matt realized it was time to move indoors, so he constructed several large vats in his basement and stored the barrels and half barrels in his garage. Demand was whopping. He found four other storage places, including his parents' barn, right across the street. He "borrowed" the Frake farm at 1227 East Lake's south side just east of Sunset Ridge. He found more hiding places in a building on the northeast corner of Harms and Glenview. A Sinclair gas station later took its place. Another secret place was in the forest preserve by Old Orchard Road between Harms Road and the river. On the west side of the paved footpath and bike trail, this location still has a round metal plate bolted down with the number 2129 on it. This covered an old hand pump for water. By the time babies two and three came along, Matt needed to make more beer to sell to the ever-expanding Glenview roadhouse market, so his home brewery concept became inconceivable. The foul-smelling fermenting odor wasn't exactly a rose garden in which to raise three young children. It probably wasn't great for the Curve's business either.

Demand for good beer spurred Matt on. He was cheered on by old Gross Point bartenders and beer peddlers who got the diddling of their lives back in 1909 when the Woman's Christian Temperance Union came in and upended their whole town. The old Gross Point guys would never surrender, and right under the WCTU's noses, they kept making and selling beer. Sadly, it wasn't the same. When the town fell apart, the Wilmette Police Department, small as it was, didn't kid around. Word was going around that the small-town bootleggers and kitchen blind pigs would only understand arrest because fines weren't stopping the ignorant immigrant Germans from drinking their demon curses.

Not entirely altruistic, as they supported their native son, the Germans just wanted some good beer. Matt up-ticked Roger Touhy's "Chicago chemist," deciding the first and most crucial ingredient for "great bier" was a professional—directly from the homeland. Letters were written and answered, and an imported brewmeister, who went by the Dutchman, helped Matt make their first business decision. They moved their beer-making process into barns in the literal backwoods of Glenview. There were a couple of locations—one on Harms Road and the other on Wagner. Trying to disguise the whole smelly process, they lined the insides of both barns with tin sheeting. The rest of the enterprise was so secret that no known recipe has ever been found. What is known is that Matt understood good, pure German bier. Since 1516, all good Germans knew there were only three crucial ingredients in bier: barley, hops and water. As the centuries moved on, the recipe was updated to include yeast. The consensus was unanimous.

"That's why the beer was so damn good. That was the best beer I ever tasted in my whole life!" said the North Shore beer drinkers who could afford it, the Germans who appreciated it and the gangsters who hunted it.

In Matt's early brewing days, Leo Schneider, Ann's brother, became Matt's partner to oversee the brewing barns. At least once, Leo took his future wife, Elsie, but left her in the car while he traipsed through the cornfields, not telling her exactly what he was up to. What little she had told her mother caused the older woman to warn her, "You better stop going with him, or you're going to get killed." (Decades later, Leo and Elsie's sons, who were part of this interview, commented that they were glad their mother didn't listen to their grandmother, or they wouldn't have been born.)

Matt's business was exploding, and a couple other friends became partners. Ed Kelly, the big guy who drove whiskey from Canada for Moran, made himself necessary to Matt. John "Andy" Andersen, a stocky guy with a red face, delivered Matt's beer to the neighborhood saloons after his real job at the pig farm. Anybody who could drive and had a truck was a bootlegger. That, and any guy who wanted extra money. You were a fool if you didn't like the money. Andy needed the dough. Newly married, he was trying to buy a place for his new bride and two baby Irish twin girls. They lived at his Catholic wife's mother's farmhouse on Waukegan Road, and Andy wasn't allowed in the house because Granny didn't like Lutherans.

Not so little anymore, Charlie Bohn bartended for Matt at his North Shore Gardens joint on Wednesdays and Friday and Saturday nights when they had music. You had to have music on the weekends because the ladies were coming to the bars now and wanted to dance. Charlie explained how to serve the setups: "The way booze was served was to keep it in the car. When some guy would come in, the charge was $2.50 for the setup, which was a bottle of ginger ale with glasses. The booze was extra—ten dollars for a quart—and then sell them the fifth or quart, whatever they wanted." Years later, Charlie worked at the Willow Inn, renamed from Henry Zeutchel's River Inn.

Matt was a spender. One time, he delivered his barrels to the Lake Street Tavern and spent his entire $150 profit, buying everyone at the bar a drink. Not that Frank minded. "In them days, those guys used to do that." Another point of view, not so congenial, was that Frank, maybe short of money, had tired of Matt's big money and big mouth, or maybe it was just a simple misunderstanding between the beer peddler and the saloon owner; the story was that Matt bought Frank's whole bar a round of drinks and lunch and then left the bill on Frank.

Gross Point's newfound son really was the big deal and an ultimate success. Apparently, beer wasn't the only thing Matt kept in those barns. Besides his dogs, his friend Max Reimer revealed that Matt had a pacer horse and a two-wheel racing cart. Max loved talking about the day he saw "crazy" Matt nestled in his little cart, the horse trotting down Glenview Road like he was a jockey at Arlington Racetrack.

Charlie Bohn remembered a story about Matt's dogs. "Boy, did I buy two nice police dogs," Matt said. "Come out and look at them." Charlie went to look at the dogs and help Matt put them in the yard, but the dogs barked and snapped like the guard dogs they were. It took the guys some natural creativity to finally put them behind the fence. Matt's dogs guarded his Waukegan Road tavern at night. In 1927 or 1928, his tavern, North Shore Gardens, burned down. Unfortunately, one of Matt's dogs died in that fire. He was heartbroken.

Heartbroken or not, it was Matt Hoffman's high-quality beer that kept Glenview in economic surplus by delivering his top-notch product to the bars, roadhouses and taverns in town while also servicing his friends' private stashes on the North Shore as he worked his way toward Chicago.

CHAPTER 4

SHOCKED, SHOCKED, DRINKING'S GOING ON

Before long, Glenview was rolling in roadhouses[39] with designations like inn, tavern, café, garden and resort. Various roadhouses included restaurants that offered "good beer, wine, and whiskey" as a resolute drawing card for customers. Chicken dinners, steaks and chops were advertised frequently. "If the liquor were removed, the large crowds would soon dwindle away." Some saloons posted signs reading, "Positively no drinking allowed," thinking they were fooling someone (like the law). Yet waiters came back and forth from a rear entrance with steins of beer and little glasses filled with liquid that looked very much like wine or whiskey.

GARDEN OF ALLAH

The Garden of Allah[40] brought a new delicacy into Glenview boundaries in the fall of 1923. The nightclub looked like something out of the Hollywood movies. In fact, it may well have been. The original Garden of Allah was a rather risqué book written in 1904, followed by several movies, the final one starring Marlene Dietrich and Charles Boyer. Built for $200,000 on the land where Lyons School stands today, the Garden of Allah was an island of pure paradise in the form of a cabaret, smack dab among the farms of Glenview. It was decorated like a Turkish villa replete with arched doorways, domed hallways, velvet drapes and luscious, private alcoves. It was said that "the kitchen was so big you could turn around in it with a Model T Ford."

The
Garden of Allah
Waukegan Road
at Glenview, Ill.

One of Glen View's most elegant restaurants was the Garden of Allah, located on the land where the Lyon School now stands. Decorated with red velvet drapes and upholstery, it was rumored to have been run by the organized crime syndicate. Old-timers told of its abrupt closure in the 1920s following the discovery of a woman's body on the patio of the establishment.

The Garden of Allah, a ritzy lounge located at the corner of present-day Lake Avenue and Waukegan Road. *Glenview History Center.*

This swanky cabaret, advertised as the "Restaurant in the Woods" and the "Show Spot of America," drew the big bands of the day. Chicken or steak dinners cost two dollars per plate, compared to diners, where one could get a burger for a quarter. Valet parkers accommodated Nash Touring cars and Rolls-Royce Phantom limousines. A taxi could be hired for seventy-five cents for a one-way trip from the Gold Coast for those on a more tender budget. In a town full of joints, roadhouses and saloons, the Garden of Allah was the exquisite swan in a sea of ugly ducklings.

Though not the Glenview type, Cy Tearney, the owner (and brother of Al Tearney, boss of a padlocked downtown speakeasy), often invited various Glenview organizations for their celebrations. On Tuesday, May 19, 1925, he hosted a dinner for the Glenview Civic Association play, *Diamonds and Hearts*. Glenview celebrities included the many Rugens (as in Richard, Ralph and Adeline), a couple Westbrooks, Nellie Synnestvedt, Dorothy Cole, Roland J. Hoffman, Arthur Palmgren, Richard Haupt, Erwin Meierhoff and Reverend M.C. Schmidt, pastor of Our Lady of Perpetual Help Church. Cyrus Tearney treated the Glenview contingency as he would have treated the star of the day, Rudolf Valentino. According to Ken Faig, it's doubtful the Glenview guests delighted in the illegal spirits that made this such a kick for some guests.

Keeping this in mind, it came as a bit of a scare when Glenview heard the news of a fire at the opulent resort on Tuesday, September 1, 1925. A porter was watching cars on the grounds when he noticed an electric light go out just before he saw fire and immediately alerted the fire department. Chief Henry Mueller rushed to the scene without sounding the fire alarm. He initially thought one of the buildings housing the help had suddenly burst into flames. After investigation, it turned out that only bedding and clothing were destroyed, probably as a result of a lighted cigarette. Chief Mueller made it clear that the siren wasn't sounded because the fire wasn't big enough to call for the equipment of the Glenview Fire Department. It must be wondered if the buildings housing the help just weren't important enough to rescue. Then there is the thought that maybe Chief Mueller had other loyalties.

The Garden of Allah knew how to delight and excite. Its summer show in 1927 showcased "Garden of Roses" by the Opera Club Orchestra under the direction of Spike Hamilton. In July 1928, Fred Hamm returned to Chicago from a solid year as a headliner on the vaudeville circuit, featured as Fred Hamm and His Collegians. That year, the dance floor was enlarged to twice its original size. Talk about Glenview growth! Memorial Day weekend in 1929 featured Jimmy Green and His Orchestra with big names Eddie Clifford, Cecille Lehman, the Ercelle Sisters, Babe Payne, Farnesworth and Vorhees and Walter Bradburg. The music was broadcasted nightly on WBBM (probably being played on the radio across the street at the Lake Street Tavern). Advertisements read, "Be convinced, and then come out to

Young people drinking the popular bootleg whiskey labeled "Old Log Cabin" imported to Chicago by Al Capone, whose trucks were hijacked by Bugs Moran. Old Log Cabin was eventually used as bait to get into Moran's headquarters, culminating in the vicious slaying of seven men in the St. Valentine's Day Massacre. *Kirn Vintage Stock/Alamy Stock Photo.*

the Garden of Allah for the perfect dance music treat." (But wait, that's not all…) "Other entertainment too!" The excitement was enough to make one wish for reverse reincarnation.

The Garden of Allah continued its road to success for the next four years. Great orchestras entertained flappers and high hats. Glenview citizens and businessmen celebrated the town's comings and goings. Fraternity boys and debutantes made this stop when home from their Ivy League colleges. As roadhouses, cafés, saloons, taverns, restaurants and soft drink parlors accumulated up and down Waukegan Road, Lake Street and other avenues, few local establishments could come close to what the Garden of Allah had to offer. The following year would bring a significant impact on Glenview police actions.

THE MILKMAN'S ON HIS WAY

Elmer Werhane, a Glenview milkman, shared a bit of a shaky story about the Garden of Allah. It seems he was driving his route and saw a car stopped and a couple of "fellows" by the big fence protecting the nightclub. Elmer pulled up and asked them, "What are you after?" The fellows responded, "We want to get into this place. We got alot [*sic*] of money, and we want to see if we can make it grow." In telling his story, Werhane said, "They had thousands of dollars. I could get them in."

The milkman really did understand the ins and outs of the security at the Garden of Allah. Not fearing sneaking in through the fence, "I went to the loose boards in the fence and gave them the password. Garden of Allah security came to the fence, their guns drawn." They addressed Werhane by a nickname, challenging him. "What do you want here, Milk?" Werhane told the security guards about the two fellows with thousands of dollars. "Okay, tell them to come in." The fellows went in, and the security frisked them. Then Werhane got back to his route. "When I came back in the daylight, the car was still there. They hadn't left all night!" His comment about coming back when it was light leaves a question as to why Werhane was driving his route in the dark and would be available to help strangers trying to break into the mob-owned hotspot. How did he happen to know about the broken boards in the fence? And how did he know the password?

THE FISHER KING[41]

Another early Glenview restaurateur, William Fischer, was ambitious and creative. In November 1923, he first opened a little grocery store on the corner of Glenview and Waukegan Roads, called the Blue and White Eat Shop. He hired Mrs. Schintzer to be the manager of what people called the Blue and White, as in, "Run to the Blue and White and pick up some Braunschweiger and pickles." The shopper could also buy canned goods, breads, cookies, cakes, butter and eggs for reasonable prices while listening to Mrs. Schintzer's Edison Victrola. In 1924, Fischer redecorated his original Blue and White Eat Shop to make it "clean shiny blue and white clear thru."

That same year, he purchased a nineteen-acre field a mile or two north on Waukegan Road. He established his Collie Exhibition Grounds, a kennel display for his white collies, chows and German police dogs. He added Fisher's Eat Shop to the property, serving everything from red-hot sandwiches to chicken dinners "at reasonable prices." On Saturday and Sunday nights, dancing and music were available in the open dining room under colored lights. Fisher (who had changed the spelling of his name) didn't miss a beat when he installed soda fountains outside and a Butter Crisp popcorn machine in the dining room. "Oh boy, Fisher's popcorn is the best ever—the faster you eat, the better it tastes." A Victrola, loudspeaker radio and electric piano entertained the diners during the week. All of this pleasure could be had without a cover charge. Fisher also rented his large dining room for wedding parties. Miss Erna E. Henze married Edward R. Gutzler, good friends of the Melzer and Dilg families, at this spot.

Bill Fisher promised a grand celebration on the Fourth of July weekend in 1924, and he did not disappoint. The nights of the fourth, fifth and sixth included dancing to a four-piece orchestra. They included fireworks as well as "ample room for parking so that one may drive off the road and stay awhile." It must have been a good summer because in 1925, Fisher erected a $25,000 dance floor, boasting it to be the largest in this part of the country. He advertised he would be adding chop suey to the menu, at a reasonable price, of course. He renamed his Fisher's Eat Shop to Fisher's Refectory and Playground. On June 4, the Glenview Bowlers informally opened the new Fisher Ballroom when they held their first annual banquet with prizes of more than $150.

On Saturday evening, June 6, 1925, they formally opened to Al Benson's "famous" orchestra for dancing on the new fifty-by-seventy-five-foot dance floor and continued on Friday, Saturday and Sunday nights. Organ music and "violano" accompanied the diners on the other nights. His menu had expanded to include a "great variety of Chinese dishes prepared by an experienced Chinese cook, so diners desiring the famous chop suey and chow mein dishes may have them served without traveling to Chicago."

A year later, Fisher reinvented himself, or at least his restaurant, and Fisher's Refectory became the Four Seasons. The reinvention included opening his ballroom to private parties. The 202nd Artillery from Fort Sheridan celebrated with 140 guests and their own military band. Another night, he hosted the Joseph M. Sesterhenn Post farewell party for the departing commander and his wife with 75 guests. The social club of Western Electric Work had a dinner dance. He also welcomed the Glenview Civic Organization of the Dramatic Club to use the Four Seasons until the Glenview Community Center was built. Mrs. Schintzer announced the dining hall availability for afternoon cards or bunco and refreshments, presumably at a reasonable price.

The man didn't miss a trick. In early September, he advertised the Four Seasons ("America's Finest Restaurant") Halloween party with dancing to a six-piece orchestra, Chinese and American food prepared by Chinese chefs and a takeout order of chop suey for fifty cents. His place was a real crowd-pleaser. One night, the cast of a local revue wound up at the Four Seasons "for a midnight frolic…and stayed till the wee sma' hours, tired as they were."

In 1926, he hired the Black Cat Orchestra on a full-time basis. Bill Fisher's hard work and extensive advertising paid off. By the summer of 1928, the Four Seasons had become an elaborate two-story edifice with a fenced garden, tall lighted columns, a second floor with striped awnings and several turrets, one topped by a flag displaying "Four Seasons." Motorists could recognize it from at least a mile in either direction, prompted by his ad, "From the North Shore suburbs, Willow or Lake St. to Waukegan Road, thence either south or north." Driving up to the "north shore's exclusive roadside resort…located in typical farm settings" was more like viewing a midsummer night's dream. Guests entered through a grand domed portico, hearing the music of Jules Novit and his orchestra. At the same time, diners purchased the special dollar dinner, dollar and a half dinners and two-dollar dinners with a choice of up to six

Advertising for one of the "Fischer King's" new restaurants. *From Daily Herald, November 2, 1923.*

courses of roast chicken, sirloin of beef or roast loin of pork, all "luscious rural foodstuffs to tempt even the most jaded appetite." In case long drive hunger pains couldn't be tamed, "barbeque stands dot the highway…. Service is provided from noon throughout the afternoon, evening and night." Besides vaudeville acts and a "galaxy of all-star performers, Four Seasons offered indoor dancing and a porch for outdoor dancing…to spend the most delightful evening reveling in the cooling breezes that sweep up from the valley." Patrons enjoyed the pleasure spectacle at a reasonable price.

Later, the name was again changed to the Black Forest. Like so many other venues, in 1933, it burned down in one of those mysterious fires.

VILLA VENICE SUPPER CLUB[42]

In 1913, the House That Jack Built was the name of an unimpressive brick roadhouse on Milwaukee Avenue, south of Willow Road. All that changed in 1921, when Albert Bouche purchased the property on the Des Plaines River. Bouche (pronounced boo-shay), born in Nice, France, arrived in Chicago in 1910 with a real knack for the restaurant and cabaret business and perhaps another knack for knowing the right people, meaning Johnny Torrio. Bouche opened the Café Belvidere at 868 North Clark and Chestnut Streets in 1915. His success and empathy for Chicago were shown with a contribution of $27.50 to the *Eastland* disaster. He was arrested on January 15, 1917, for failure to observe the Sunday closing rule, but seemed to escape any sort of punishment, perhaps due to a Torrio connection. In May 1917, he opened Moulin Rouge Gardens, replacing Rainbo Gardens at Clark and Lawrence as a summer resort with vaudeville shows and dinners going late into the night. He moved Moulin Rouge Gardens to 416 South Wabash and stayed open all year as a true impresario. He really knew what he was doing when he decided to make the little property on the Des Plaines River a state-of-the-art cabaret. It didn't seem to matter that it was Prohibition. Perhaps it helped that it was Glenview. Perhaps it also helped that Torrio and Capone had their hands in Bouche's success by now. In a 1923 raid of local roadhouses, it was reported that "the House that Jack Built drew a blank."

Bouche was well known among the Chicago high hats. This restaurateur deserved his reputation and turned this unassuming roadhouse into a "Rendezvous for the Discriminating." He charged $2.50 for his dinners and no cover charge if the dinner guests arrived before 9:00 p.m. The master advertiser even added a little line at the bottom assuring guests that "the roads would be patrolled for automobiles."

He advertised that in leaving nothing to the imagination, he spent $100,000 to "entertain Chicagoans, North Shore, and smart suburban sets as the finest summer resort." The steady supply of good liquor was an essential part of the entertainment for college boys, debutantes[43] and sporting men of the wealthy class. On June 12, 1924, one of Villa Venice's grand openings promoted thirty-five New York artists in $15,000 costumes, advising, "Come on and See What New York or Any Other Larger City Hasn't Got!" This was confirmed by an article in a local magazine styled like the *New Yorker*, which reported the interests of the high-hat and silk-stocking elites in Chicago. Gene Markey of the *Chicagoan* wrote:

> *On Milwaukee Road* [sic] *you will arrive at the Villa Venice, which if I may say so, is the ultimate, the last word, the nirvana of Cook County estaminets. Its grounds, superbly landscaped into gardens such as no roadhouse ever boasted before, lead down to the banks of the Desplaines* [sic]*, where an imported gondola waits; within the villa, service, and cuisine are admirable, the band is excellent, and at nine and midnight Mr. Albert Bouche's[44] European revue comes on. New York has never known a country inn and amusement place like the Villa Venice.*

Villa Venice provided elegant dining outside in its famous garden. *Courtesy Northbrook Historical Society.*

Bouche's Villa Venice famous Venetian gondola scene. *Courtesy J.W. Craig, undereverytombstone. blogspot.com.*

BOUCHE'S VILLA VENICE, FAMOUS VENETIAN GONDOLA SCENE

There was no end to his creative thoughts. The dreamland was reached like an adult Disneyland by driving through a white arched entry into formal Venetian gardens accented with twinkle lights and water fountains. In the summer of 1925, he thought gondolas would give some pizzazz to his already elegant and alluring venue. Forced to negotiate with the Italian government for permission, he intended to buy original antique Venetian gondolas, which were piloted by "chanting gondoliers." It's not known if the gondoliers were antique, Venetian or authentic.

He originally opened the Villa Venice as a summer resort, giving him the freedom to travel to Europe, South America and his favorite travel spot, Cuba, searching for fresh talent and new ideas for his shows. In his travels for new talent, he advertised for five-foot-eight-inch girls. His phone rang relentlessly by young dancers anxious to work for the man who would become the Ziegfeld of floor shows. Every night, there were three shows: at nine o'clock, midnight and 2:45 a.m. The first and last productions were the same, but a new spectacle prompted his customers to stay for the second show at midnight.

In 1927, looking for a new emcee with a comical bent, he interviewed and turned down Bob Hope, saying, "You won't do," and then Bouche bought him a steak. As the 1930s arrived, Sally Rand performed her fan dance while guests watched, eating excellent cuisine and, probably most welcome, enjoying the latest cooling system. In 1928, Al Copeland's orchestra provided the music for dancing and the comedy *Vagaries of 1928*, which, besides its actors, included "ten beautiful dancing darlings."

By the time the 1930s arrived, Bouche spent more time in Miami Beach. He opened another Villa Venice and declared himself the "Papa of All Nite Clubs." On October 12, 1956, the *Chicago Daily Tribune* sadly reported,

"Aging Papa Bouche sold his Villa Venice and poof goes Chi's most fantastic showplace." It seemed the days when guests felt they had been magically transported to the Italian Riviera were over.

I Saw a Man Dance with His Wife[45]

Fast-forward to 1960, when some power brokers, one of them silent owner Sam Giancana, got hold of the site and spent over $250,000 to restore it. The walls and ceilings were lined with satin. In Giancana's quest for déjà vu, lanterns on the Des Plaines River lighted the gondola rides. Waiters and doormen attended to crowded patrons in the eight-hundred-seat room. During the shows, cameras were constantly flashing to catch the lightly clothed darlings on the stage. Last but not least, ladies of the evening were available for gentlemen who desired feminine company.

Frank Sinatra and the Rat Pack starred in seven days of shows in November–December 1962. Eddie Fisher, Sammy Davis Jr. and Dean Martin opened for the main attraction. The nightclub made $275,000 to $300,000, a record haul. What made these superstars come all the way to little old Glenview? It was said that Sam Giancana wanted payback for doing his part in the John Kennedy election. It truly became the House That Jack Built. After the Rat Pack left, the Villa Venice went downhill, reduced to a catering hall. New owners took over in 1965, and in March 1967, it was destroyed by—guess what?—another one of those mysterious fires.

Shanties in Old Shanty Town[46]

A Grand dance will be held in the Grove Pavilion, Milwaukee and Lake Avenue, 1 mile south of Des Plaines River bridge, Sunday evening, June 3, at 8:30 o'clock P.M. new time. Very latest up-to-date music furnished. Refreshments served. Good order maintained.

It's questionable if the "good order maintained" was a proposal to a good party and revelers should BYOB or a warning that the grand dance was to be dry. Whatever it was, people just wanted to have fun.

According to "Milkman" Elmer Werhane, Glenview neighbor Mr. Halavin owned the first ice cream parlor in the area on the northeast corner of Harms and what is now Old Orchard Road. He charged ten cents for a scoop and a small cone. He demanded a little more for a sandwich and a beer, as the place was a front for a blind pig. Across Harms Road from Halavin's, in the forest preserve, was a large saloon with a dance hall run by a fellow named Anderson. The saloon was set back in the woods so no one could hear what was going on. People wondered how Anderson was able to build back there because it was on forest preserve property. Nick Biederer lived around the corner from Halavin's. "He [Halavin] was a stocky guy who looked like his head was stuck on top of his shoulders and built like a bulldog." Nick would rather fight than eat. He never brought a girl, but when he went to the dances, he always found a girl. This bar "was a knockout—it was terrible!" The last dance at this saloon ended in a beer bottle fight. A person like Nick would break off the bottom of a bottle and come after you with it. "I guess two or three were killed that time....During Prohibition, they must of [sic] buried a lot of them in the forest preserve."

Fred and Al Krueger[47] sold their original place, Krueger's Hall, on Glenview and Waukegan Road, to Henry Dusing and Mr. Berg, who moved from Chicago. Renaming it the Glenview Inn, they changed it into a large dining room with a dance hall with a four-piece orchestra on Monday and Tuesday nights. It was big enough to hold the American Legion dance on February 9, 1924. Four days later, they were able to feature it as the

The northeast corner of Glenview and Waukegan Roads, originally owned and operated by William Haut. Notice the Glenview Inn, the white building to the left. *Erwin Meierhoff photo from "Roots: A Glenview Story."*

Glenview Theatre and show the latest comedy, *The Man Next Door*. For fifty cents, anyone could attend the opening, a benefit dance given by the God Fellowship Club to honor Officer Shaefer of Wilmette, who recently got out of the hospital. The Glenview Inn also hosted an American Legion dance. This was another place that could be open at all hours, as Mr. Berg lived in an adjoining flat.

There were some honest ice cream parlors, such as Noffz, with a fine new soda fountain and a dark green linoleum floor. Noffz was on the south side of Glenview Road, almost next door to the Blue Heron. Paul Kretz opened Ice Cream Parlor and Lunch Room, providing day and night service on Waukegan and Glenview.

In May 1924, the Krueger brothers bought the restaurant from John Wenzel across from Matt Hoffman's North Shore Gardens on Waukegan and Chestnut. Fred Krueger and his wife lived in the house adjoining, allowing her to "cook meals at any hour for hungry motorists." Fred had a radio to get news and programs from New York and Chicago, and he kept "the *Cook County Herald* to get all the most important home news for 25 miles around." Their brother Ernie had a place on the corner of Waukegan and Glenview Roads. Matt Hoffman sold to all of them.

MEIER'S TAVERN[48]

It wasn't just Waukegan Road snagging all the roadhouse business. Frank Meier had been eyeing his buddies and the growing saloon situation with interest—probably moneyed interest. His business, the Wilmette Ice Company, was literally drowning. Restaurants and homeowners needed ice deliveries like they needed another lemonade. Besides that, Frank knew a good beer peddler: Matt Hoffman.

In 1924, Frank and Anna Meier and their eight children moved out of their Washington Street home in Wilmette and bought a little farmhouse on the east end of Lake Avenue. From the infamous, bankrupt and sadly departed Gross Point, thirsty old friends and family flocked to his new place. Initially, Frank and Anna invited a few friends to join them in their living room for dime beers and a fifteen-cent burger. The year wasn't up before Frank and Anna had to add on to their living room, turning it into a Saturday night speakeasy. The new addition included little doorbells by some of the tables so the parched customers could ring for immediate hydration.

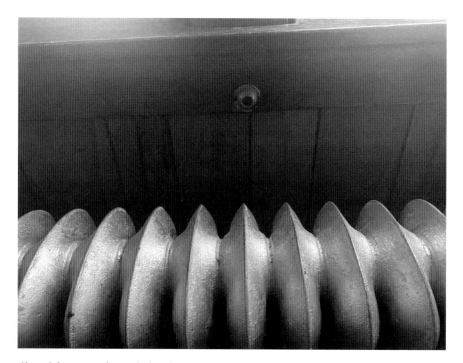

Above: A buzzer under a window (and over a radiator) at Meier's Tavern, presumably to order a drink but possibly an alarm to signal the management about unwanted "guests." *Jill Ruschli Crane Collection.*

Opposite, top: Meier's Tavern. Nothing has changed much, although the pony rink is gone. *From* Glenview, the First Centennial.

Opposite, bottom: Meier's Tavern dressed for the holidays and welcoming for almost a century. *Jill Ruschli Crane Collection.*

Frank Meier ran a respectable establishment. Because his wife worked with him and wanted the ladies to feel comfortable, if not actually dignified, he devised a little plan to keep the gasbags in line. Suppose some fool was to curse, swear or utter profanities, even if it just slipped out of his mouth after a few pops. In that case, it was going to cost him the price of another beer—ten cents into the tip jar for every foul-mouthed utterance. And the money in the tip jar? Frank might have used it to buy his wife carnations on their wedding anniversary. This little fact made news in 1925. After all, Meier's Tavern was a family joint. He encouraged the families, especially the fathers who never had enough time to spend with their kids. Frank came up with an idea to keep the little ones busy. Nickels poured into his cash register for the bored kids sitting idle on barstools in an adult land

where TVs and iPads hadn't yet been invented. He built a pony rink right outside the tavern, mere feet from their doting, drinking parents. Frank raked out a little clearing and talked to his buddy Andy Andersen to help him buy a couple old Shetlands. He tethered the horses to the arms of the pony wheel with weaver halter ropes and cinches. The little innocents sat on their miniature saddles as the little pony went round and round at a speed of about a tenth of a mile an hour.

No saloon in Glenview could compete with that. So, while adults drank their beers, their kiddos scrambled for a seat on their favorite pony at a time when restaurants were either high-end nightspots or little breakfast diners. According to someone with authentic insight, Jim Masterson, owner of Hackney's, appreciated Frank Meier's idea right from the horse's mouth. In the little free time he had, he enjoyed watching his seven kids have a good time in one of the few places in Glenview where children were actually welcome. Everyone was happy. Especially Frank and Anna.

In 1960, they called it a day and sold the place. Twenty-nine years passed like nothing, and then it was purchased by Gus Pappas, the fourth owner. Frank still stopped by, and every so often, he'd serve a patron a beer until he died in 2004. Almost one hundred years later, the unassuming roadhouse hasn't changed much. Lake Street got busier, the pony rink was gone and prices increased, but the décor was original. So original that Aaron Spelling took pictures and re-created the bar for one of his TV shows. Who would have thought Frank and Anna Meier's little speakeasy would turn Hollywood?

A Little Raid Here and There[49]

The year 1924 brought more little roadhouses and blind pigs to Glenview. In June, forty-two Prohibition agents busted eight roadhouses and arrested twenty-six people. They seized almost eight hundred gallons of wine, whiskey and moonshine. They confiscated fifty barrels of beer, along with twenty-five cases of gin and other cordials. Most of the arrests were of college students celebrating the weekend in "gin parties." The Glenview roadhouses, counting their losses, included that of the Krueger brothers on Waukegan Road. Down the street, Koehne's Tavern was also raided, as was Julius Meyers's.

A year later, three Glenview roadhouses were newly licensed by the quick-thinking Cook County legislature trying to reap some of the monetary benefits the gangs did. It goes without saying, no matter how much money the county collected, they couldn't possibly amass in a decade the gobs of money the gangs racked up in a day. Frank Engels was granted a license for the Lake Avenue Tavern. The other two were for the Willow Inn with a new name and a new owner, Patrick deMicheil, and Villa Venice, owned by Albert Bouche.

The Glenview police might not have bothered the saloons, but the feds could not be trusted. "A raid in November 1925, by prohibition officers out

A raid on a home that served as a distribution warehouse for illegal liquor. The next question is how the agents are going to get all those cartons in that little truck. *The Protected Art Archive/Alamy Stock Photo.*

Glenview way, netted several arrests and much alcohol. One Glenview man became indignant when he was arrested, claiming that he was a member of a certain political organization and had paid his dues, so he should be protected from the raids. The raiders did not recognize the membership card but took five gallons of alcohol away."[50]

THAT AGE-OLD GLENVIEW QUESTION: WHICH HACKNEY'S CAME FIRST? HARMS OR LAKE?[51]

In 1919, Betty and Ed Masterson owned a little roadhouse at Clark and Narragansett, where they raised their children, four-year-old Jim and his younger sister, Helen. Barely a year later, Ed died of black lung disease, leaving Mama Betty, only thirty-one years old, with two babies to raise and a bar to run. Prohibition squealed in, pouring a little extra salt in Widow Betty's wounds.

Frank Engels changed all that. Frank, a grandson of the Gross Point Engels family, immigrants from Trier, Germany, in the 1840s, liked the saloon business, especially because Betty was so good at it. In 1924, they married and purchased a small parcel of land just east of Waukegan Road on Lake Street in Glenview. They built themselves a home for Betty's little ones upstairs while they crafted the street level into a small speakeasy that they named the Lake Avenue Tavern.

In those early days, Betty chopped her own beef, cooked, cleaned and kept the books, all the while raising little Jim and Helen. Pure steel but dainty too, the woman created a gold mine with well-prepared food, rich beer and fair prices. Glenview and Gross Point businessmen and farmers welcomed the new place. Due to the profusion of the latest automobiles and because people liked taking rides, Frank and Betty soon had customers from all along the North Shore and into Chicago. Yes, they served alcohol. Yes, it was Prohibition. Glenview didn't mind. Frank and Betty poured a good amount of economic prosperity into their new home village, with the village taking little risk and the Engels family taking it all.

Speaking of risk, a fine little tale circulated about Betty from her good friend who saw her in action. Mary Kelly gabbed about an afternoon when a couple of punks showed up at the tavern. Betty was given the standard plug-ugly order to "give them all her money," while Mary squished herself under a table. Betty might have been slim, fair and quite frail (in the day's vernacular), but she was no slacker. She threw up her skinny arms, one of them holding her meat-chopping cleaver. She wielded her newfound battleaxe inches from one of the faces of those stupid dopes and told them to get the hell out. Boy, did they amscray, like bullets out of a gun. Some stupid anti-feminists said it was because she was a woman. Even the vilest thieves had too much respect to attack a woman. Mary, her jittery friend under the table, wished Betty's courage could have been contagious. However, it seemed Mary was not apt to catch it. More than a half-century later, the people at Hackney's had never heard the story. Could it be that Mary was just a natural flimflammer?

HACKNEY'S ON HARMS[52]

In 1925, Betty's sister Helen, nicknamed Bebe, met a hunky Irishman named Jack Hackney, a bartender at the Green Parrot, a sweet little saloon at Grace Street and Seminary, who became the love of her life. Wanting out

Betty Engels and Bebe Hackney posing at an ironic photo set at Riverview. Ironic in that Jack and Bebe owned a back-porch bar on Harms Road. *Courtesy of Mary Welch, Hackney's on Harms.*

The original Hackney's on Harms where Jack and Bebe started their restaurant. This is the same home that housed Jim and Kitz Masterson and their seven children. Liz Masterson Hebson says the kids would ask their mom where dinner was, and some nights she would say, "The tavern," meaning the little cabin on the left. *Jill Ruschli Crane Collection*.

Left to right: Unknown; unknown; Kitz Masterson holding son Ed; Jim Masterson petting Jip the dog; Julie Wickboldt, the cook; unknown soldier. The little girl in the snowsuit and white shoes is Liz Masterson Hebson. *Courtesy of Mary Welch, Hackney's on Harms.*

of Chicago's dust and dirt, they married and purchased a little farmhouse in Glenview about a mile from Betty and Frank and her little ones. It being Prohibition, Jack being a bartender and their house being isolated, making beer seemed to be the thing to do. They put their new home to work by giving away corned beef sandwiches and selling beer with the food for a nickel. The little watering hole was fashioned out of their glassed-in back porch under a Hamm's sign. German farmers flocked from nearby Wilmette, deprived of their own bars thanks to 1909 temperance laws. Pretty soon, the newlywed Hackneys had a good thing going, just like the Engels family. Fond of her German clientele and reminiscent of her German roots in the form of the German cook who took care of the girls after their mother died, Bebe got the idea to fry hamburgers in bacon grease in a ten-inch black iron frying pan.

Just like in the old country, on Sundays, the German wives and kids joined the husbands for picnics in the Hackneys' big backyard on Harms Road. It wasn't long before the Hackneys had to enlarge their operation and extend their garage to accommodate a four-stool bar, an office and an "inventory room" to store their liquor. With their newfound customers, more space and Matt Hoffman's beer, the hardworking Hackneys won their little slice of success. As business continued picking up, Jack and Bebe made a corporate decision to charge a quarter for a burger on Bebe's homemade dark rye, which would one day become the famous Hackneyburger®.

Nearly one hundred years later, both restaurants are still full of life. Mike Welch, great-grandson of pretty Betty Masterson, followed his dream, with the help of his wife, Megan, and founded Macushla, a pioneer brewery in the back of the original Lake Avenue Tavern. This labor of love—as shown in its name, which means "my pulse, my lifeblood, my darling"—is alive in its spirit of the past and the present. Young Mike died near the first anniversary of his passion. Megan now runs the brewery, flourishing even during Covid years, successfully keeping the century-old traditions on the map in Glenview.

THE KELLY CLAN COASTS INTO GLENVIEW

One day in dusty 1921, after her husband died, Sarah Kelly sold the Half Day Inn. She told the neighbors her handsome sweetheart died of gout and then buried her roadhouse fortune in her homemade coat pocket, along with her grief. She left behind the graves of twin girls and her oldest and youngest, dead from scarlet fever. Grown now, her surviving son and two daughters packed up their old Model T with their baggage and the better furniture. The misshapen family drove south down Waukegan Road looking like the Jed Clampett caravan coasting into Beverly Hills. Waukegan Road, being no Sunset Strip, was scrutinized by each traveling Kelly for a fresh

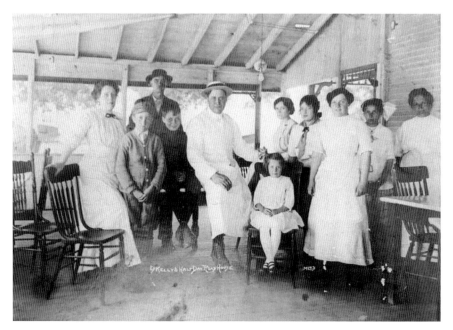

The Kelly family at the Half Day Inn, circa 1913. *Left to right:* Sarah Kelly; young Ed Kelly; unknown standing man; unknown young boy; Ed Kelly in white, holding hands with daughter Mary (wearing a tie). The little girl in the white dress, sitting in the chair, is Grace Kelly. The others are unknown and assumed to be staff. *Jill Ruschli Crane Collection.*

opportunity in a new home. Near Glenview by Lake Avenue, they spotted a frame house and bought it on the spot. Seventy years later, the land would be the site of Maryhaven. At that moment, though, they were the beginning of a newly arrived family in Glenview, Illinois, certainly not like the Hutchings, Dewes or Rugen families emigrating from across the ocean. But this broken family also worked hard, suffered and gave Glenview the roots and diversity that make the village what it is.

SARAH'S ROSARY

They moved into their new home, scrubbing and cleaning and, all the while, Sarah saying the rosary. She had the most unusual and uncanny ability to move her rosary lips and, at the same time, shout out directives to her household, ordering them to find real jobs. Ed became a truck farmer. Mary went to Chicago's Loop and found a job in Marshall Fields, "giving the ladies what they wanted"—in her case, hats. Young Grace took the train with Mary to work for Dr. Grimmer, a popular homeopathic doctor. Ed shared his third-story attic room with Sarah's source of income, boarders. To their core, they thought of themselves as lace curtain Irish, proud, frugal, hardworking and American.

As the Roaring Twenties ended, something strange happened to Sarah. She lost her grip. Whatever grit she had fled. She explained that her heart tittered too much, beat too hard and burst through her chest. With no positive diagnosis of a health problem, her anxiety forced her to her room and finally to her bed, shouting orders and kneading her rosary beads until she wore them out.

Rosary beads rarely met the painted fingers of Sarah's daughters. Mary and Grace cut their hair and rouged their cheeks. They got rid of their horrifyingly tight corsets, another useless bind on their freedom. They rolled up their skirts, loosened their dresses and celebrated their fresh air with a good drag on their cigarettes. If need be, they told you where to get off with their newfound "man" language spurting out of their painted lips. They went to saloons and met men. No wonder Sarah stayed in bed and prayed her rosary.

GLENVIEW FLAPPERS[53]

Mary and Grace were independent girls who took the train to their jobs in Chicago's Loop. Ed would pick his sisters up at the end of their day, and the three siblings would stop at a nearby roadhouse for a little set-up. Ed always had a full flask and a lot of good friends at these drink houses. Herb Rugen's Soft Drink Parlor was the closest to the train. After a pop or two, they'd swing by the Cozy Inn just down Grove Street on Waukegan. It was too bad when Glenview president McCullen closed it down for disorderly conduct. When Alfred Koehne built the Glenview Inn next to John Dilg's place, they were the first ones there. Their city girlfriends, anxious to sow some wild oats—not the farm kind—joined Mary and Grace on the train to Glenview, especially on Fridays.

One of the girls, Mary Ryan, born of a sharp German mother, lived in luxury on Congress Parkway. Grace met Mary on their way to lunch one day as Mary explained she worked in a urologist's office down the hall. Gossiping on those Friday nights at the Glenview roadhouses, Mary Ryan tittered about her boss, who happened to have as a patient the unctuous mob boss Al Capone. After a cocktail or two, Mary Ryan got a kick out of telling her friends about procedures the doctor performed on the syphilis-ridden gangster that involved his male nonmentionable and the doctor's needles. Grace Kelly, ever delightful and never rude, pointed out that the squatty Scarface should go to Dr. Grimmer. His homeopathic philosophy, popular in the '20s, was to give the body a little of what's wrong with it and let the body fight it off with its own antibodies. All it took was to put a few sugar pills under their tongues.

More and more, Mary Ryan joined the Kelly sisters on Fridays. They

were steady guests at the Blue Heron, Haut's, Hoffman's and John Dilg's place, where they could dance all night. Who cared what else mattered when a girl stood on a good dance floor with a good orchestra and a good crowd? Of course, it helped if there were good men and no fuss buddies to lend a disapproving eye. The girlfriends loved the Charleston and the eccentric two-step. Just thinking about it could send chills up their spines.

Advertising for Koehne's Tavern. *From* Daily Herald, *November 2, 1923.*

The Roaring Twenties was in its heyday, as was Glenview, when the girls designated themselves

Original caption: "New York: repeal Shoes…For The New Fall Season. With the new craze for wine and liquor shades of footwear, these two numbers are certain to prove enormously popular. The shades are Port wine (*left*) and champagne and made their appearance at a recent advance showing of the shoe and leather industry." Women drank in public during Prohibition. *Courtesy Bettmann/Getty Images.*

"The Girls." The Girls and Ed tried Fisher's Restaurant and the Casino. Some nights, they'd find a small cabaret-style singing quartet where a girl sang the most popular songs. They would all swoon and sing along, and it helped when Ed Kelly tipped well. There were so many places to go, the weekend was never long enough. They wished they could go to Garden of Allah and Villa Venice, but they were pretty much out of their price range, even if they might meet a wealthy gangster. That was always Mary Kelly's hope. If he was in town, Ed Kelly continued to pick the Girls up at the train. If he was traveling, it was no problem; they danced, drank, smoked and giggled. It seemed that Ed was gone more than they wished, but Ed had a good job with Bugs Moran, and that revelation turned them on.

> *Dry Raiders Seize Liquor Worth $12,000 at Glenview. Prohibition agents late last night raided a roadhouse conducted by William Haut in Glenview, Ill. and seized liquor valued at $12,000. It was the biggest seizure of contraband ever made in a roadhouse in the Chicago district, according to the agents.*

The Girls loved it and felt like they were celebrity molls, as Haut's place was one of their weekend hangouts. William's son Al, apparently not as impassioned as the Girls regarding gang activity, decided not to take over the family business and opened a funeral home farther north on Waukegan Road.

As Prohibition neared its tenth year, Capone started to make a stronger presence in Glenview. It didn't take more than a year for the Moran gang to be crippled after the St. Valentine's Day massacre. Bugs Moran was not the sharpest tool in the box (though it didn't matter to him, as he was still of the opinion that the biggest, fastest, toughest gun won). He quit trying to hold on to his own turf and eventually left the suburbs for the faraway Lake County toward the state line. Roger Touhy was as happy as a clam, making forty-five clams on each barrel of beer, happier still to be able to give it to the police organizations that protected him, as long he kept prostitution out of their townships, but mostly happy because Moran hobbled out of his way, setting up the perfect opportunity to finally exploit Matt Hoffman.

The Girls usually seemed to wind up their night at the Lake Avenue Tavern, almost across the street from Mary and Grace's house. Mary Kelly loved the saloon life, so it wasn't odd for her to stop by during the week. She adored Betty Engels, the little bundle who never stopped working. Andy Andersen was the Lake Street Tavern beer delivery man or, in 1920s terms, bootlegger. No offshoot of her rosary-instilled mother, the underworld life enchanted Mary. What she saw in Andy Andersen was not a hardworking cattleman who drove a truck to cop a couple hundred bucks. Mary was looking to marry a large chunk of money, and Bugs Moran, a big personality who drove a fast car, wore tailored clothes and took a girl to swanky places, was her guy. Unfortunately, Moran, never one to pass up a good shot, might have thought Mary the cat's pajamas, but it was his wife he was committed to. Mary looked at her next best thing—short, squat Andy Andersen, who was no more her type than Bella Lugosi. Mary married fantasy Andy, and within a year, they had two baby girls who didn't look at all alike. Bedbound Sarah banished the Lutheran Andy Andersen from her house. She may have been bedridden, but she also had all the money. The little Andersen Irish twins, Jane and Bette (named for Mary's meat-slinger friend at the Lake Avenue Tavern), became part and parcel of the Kelly clan on Waukegan Road. It wasn't too long before their father would have to flee for his life, leaving the tots in misery and misunderstanding.

Villa del Mar[54]

In 1928, John G. Adinamis built a Spanish-looking restaurant and bar, Villa Del Mar, on property he purchased in 1926. Located on the corner next to the Lake Street Tavern, he attracted the town's original families, the Rugens, Synnestvedts and Claveys. Famous patrons stopped by, such as Ennio Bolgnini, world-renowned cellist; Amelia Earhart; and Jimmy Doolittle, who came with the air races in 1930. John's son Dean took a set of urns from the front of the closed-down Garden of Allah and added them to the front of his restaurant, saving a little piece of the former nightclub's heyday.

In August 1936, Fred Schneider, a bartender in "a nearby tavern," saw a car run down two young sons of the corner gas station operator. Schneider ran out, jumped on the running board of a nearby passing car and ordered the driver to follow the hit-and-run killers. It was a fast three miles south on Waukegan Road before they finally caught up with drunk drivers, who told Morton Grove police they "had just a couple beers" in Lake County. "He 'realized he had hit something but didn't know what it was and kept on driving.'" Although the eight-year-old boy was killed and his six-year-old brother injured, Fred Schneider was still a hero.

Until the roadhouse business in Glenview got too big, Matt Hoffman sold his beer freely in Glenview, a small part of Bugs Moran's territory. It's assumed other gangs stayed away, not realizing Moran was more concerned with

Exterior of Villa Del Mar in 1928 at Glen Oak Shopping Center on the northeast corner of Lake and Waukegan. It was owned by the John Adinamis family. Notice the urns at the entrance from Garden of Allah. Not shown is a gas station at this corner. *From* Glenview, the First Centennial.

extorting money from the Cleaners and Dye Unions and using Al Capone for a shooting gallery. Matt's customers weren't even called customers; they were called friends at his couple or twenty joints. Matt stayed away from the joints where "the Boys" supplied the booze, like the Garden of Allah and Villa Venice. It wasn't that he was afraid of them. To be honest, Matt didn't even think about it, secure in Moran's lackadaisical power and imperious to his own naivete. There was another guy who wanted Matt's business, and that would be Matt's undoing.

CHAPTER 5

IT'S ALL ABOUT THE GOOD HOOCH

T he Glenview fathers were buzzing along,[55] careful with finances and campaigning for worthwhile improvements in their thirty-year-old town. At a village meeting in May 1928, the Glenview Civic Association picked up the tab for new street signs. Frank Rugen pointed out, "They are the best that can be purchased and will last practically indefinitely." It's not known if any of the old signs are still in existence, in which case they would have lasted almost one hundred years, proving Frank right. The other good news, as the best was saved for last, was about constructing a new civic building. It was to be built on the property where the old Glenview Days was held (now Jackman Park). The lowest bid for the facility that would serve as the Village Hall came in from Joe Zander Builders. There was no discussion of saloons, roadhouses or alcoholic beverages.

Also buzzing along were at least thirty roadhouses, saloons, nightclubs, restaurants, soft drink parlors and whatever else kind of place was opened for those wanting a bit to eat and maybe a little glow.

TROUBLE BREWING IN GLENVIEW[56]

In November 1928, the *Chicago Tribune* reported that at eleven o'clock in the morning, two cars drove up to the Lake Street Tavern and opened the door, and five hoods jolted Betty with aimed pistols and violently ordered her upstairs to wake Frank. After forcing him to open the safe, they stole $1,500 in valuables and tied up the nervous owners. Due to a case of bad timing, a North Shore couple popped in, expecting a pleasant lunch, and instead were bound and robbed. The gang told them "'not to give an alarm' and vanished without a clew [*sic*] to their identity or the direction of their escape." There was no indication this robbery was resolved. That's how it was in out-of-the-way roadhouses in those days. But Betty and Frank kept plugging on.

CAPONE MOVES IN[57]

Al Capone was tiptoeing his way into the northern suburbs with his size-seven shoes and his thug capos. He tried moving a saloon and a bordello into Schiller Park, Roger Touhy's land. That didn't last long. Touhy got a few guys to tear that place apart. Violence was finding its way to the northern suburbs and, sadly, Glenview.

In late 1927, Al Capone, short of beer because of police shutdowns of his breweries, gave Roger a call. Hustle would be a better word, but it was just the beginning of the many confrontations. Capone wanted to make a deal with Roger Touhy for five hundred gallons of his "high quality" beer. Touhy agreed, saying he was long on beer. He even gave Capone a discount, charging him only $37.50 a barrel, a considerable bargain from the usual $55.00. After Capone received the beer, he immediately called Roger back to complain, "Fifty barrels were leakers." "Bull-ogny," as they say in Italian, Roger spat back, with stronger words. Obviously, the mob boss was trying to swindle him. Roger was such a perfectionist about every inch of his operation, including the barrels. It was like those barrels were his sons. He wasn't going to let this crook get away with jack.

Bugs Moran[58] kept tracking Capone down with his elaborate and destructive shooting wars. Moran loved his guns, his fancy car, dressing well and terrorizing Capone. He was a big buck with a unique spiritual direction in that he also loved his new wife and adopted her son, John. He was crazy about that kid and constantly bought him gifts. What really bugged Moran was Capone's pursual of prostitution. There was no room on the North Side territory for that nasty kind of bawdiness. By the end of 1928, Moran realized he had made a tactical error when he pushed Canadian whiskey on his friends in the saloons for a more than healthy profit. The problem was that his people liked Old Log Cabin. When Moran realized his mistake, he simply hijacked other gangs' trucks for the popular whiskey and made even more money. It was better to peddle booze at exorbitant prices and shake

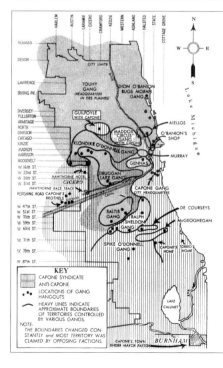

Amid the smoke of the finest Havanas the bloodstained brigands sliced up the city of Chicago. Map shows a 1926 division of the spoils. Later Al Capone had the gall to suggest that I serve as arbiter for another gangland realignment of territories.

Above: Rival gang bosses Al Capone and George "Bugs" Moran. *Courtesy Everett Collection Historical/Alamy Stock Photo.*

Left: The Chicago gang map. Notice all the Roger Touhy territory. *From* The Dry and Lawless Years.

down dry-cleaning shops and unions. So successful were his shakedowns of cleaning businesses and unions that the Chicago Master Cleaners and Dyers Association had to announce the quality of its representation with a published statement of mishandled "facts."

The St. Valentine's Day Massacre[59]

Capone had enough of Moran and literally shot his wad on the 1929 Valentine's Day Massacre. Too bad for Capone that Bugs didn't get the memo. The simplicity of Scarface's scheme had one of his men pretend to be an Old Log Cabin hijacker. It only took a couple of "stolen" shipments to gain Moran's trust and execute part two of Capone's clever plan. He hired some unrecognizable torpedoes from New York to set up a lookout

Original caption: "Gangster hideout across from slaying scene in Chicago Illinois. This is a view of the 2100 block of North Clark Street, Chicago. The building on the extreme right is the rooming house where gangsters under assumed names rented a room to spy on the S.M.C. Cartage garage, where Moran gangsters hung out, police believe. The Cartage garage is on the left of the photo between the laundry sign and tailor shop sign." *Courtesy Bettmann/Getty Images*.

Gruesome photo of the interior of SMC Cartage on February 14, 1929, after a fake police raid turned into the massacre of the Moran gang. The hired torpedoes from out of town mistook another gangster for Moran, who happened to be walking toward the garage at the time. When he saw the police cars, he passed by the "raid," which saved his life. *Courtesy Everett Collection Historical/Alamy Stock Photo.*

across from Moran's booze headquarters, SMC Cartage on Clark Street. It was foolproof. The faux hijacker called Moran with another faux shipment. Could he deliver the goods at 10:30 a.m. on February 14? The guys in the windows across the street set their watches. Being strangers in the Second City, they had never seen Moran and didn't know him from Adam, so they were given a picture of Moran, and as soon as he showed up, another phone call would be made. After seeing various North Siders enter the building on that lightly snowy St. Valentine's Day, they waited, apparently impatiently, until they saw their guy. A big man in an overcoat, just like the picture, walking with a friend, went through the door, and the plan went into action. In no time, a police car drove up, and four cops busted through the door of SMC Cartage. Ordered to line up against the wall, the North Siders figured it was just another raid and undoubtedly hoped the cops would be quick and the delivery would be late. At this exact time, Bugs Moran, a little late, was making his way to the garage, saw the police and just kept walking. In

Crowds outside the SMC Cartage garage on February 14, 1929, after the infamous slaughter of the Moran gang, aka the St. Valentine's Day Massacre. Young Ed Kelly was in the crowd counting his blessings that he was running late that day to pick up and distribute booze for Moran. *Courtesy Chicago History Museum/Getty Images. Photo by* Chicago Sun-Times/ Chicago Daily News Collection.

the garage, seven men and a dog were sprayed with machine-gun bullets. Only the dog survived. Capone was notified and was overjoyed. Then it was discovered the thugs had observed the wrong man. It goes to show, you can't depend on outsiders to do your dirty work.

Detective Chief John Stege declared that the killers were "out-of-town assassins" who had been paid by the head. The more Moran men they murdered, the more money they made. The figure reported by Stege was $10,000 per dead body. Everyone was horrified. Capone couldn't believe his miserable misfortune. Politicians were outraged. The good people of Chicago had had enough. "Stop the shooting," they ordered their alderman. Finally, Moran was truly scared and checked himself into St. Francis Hospital for a few days. After that, he went to Windsor, Canada, and hopped a boat to Paris. He would have to figure out what to do. Ed Kelly, Moran's hired bootlegger, was in the auspicious position to be a couple hours short of being killed that bloody day. As his luck would have it, he was one of the guys on the pickup end. Once the shipment got into the warehouse, Ed would come in with his truck, pick up a load for his drums in Glenview and get the hell out of there. The deal with Ed was he was always late. Really late. He liked to have a few snorts. He talked a lot. He slept late. It saved his life that day.

GARDEN OF ALLAH[60]

It was eight o'clock in the morning of September 4, 1929, when eight racketeers invaded the nightclub through the kitchen. Only the cook and the chef were working when the bandits ordered the two to open the safe. As the two were useless at that task, the bandits, bright people that they were and knowing a losing game when they saw one, fielded their guns and went to wake up the boss. Cy Tearney was sleeping soundly in his tiny apartment upstairs over the kitchen. A restaurateur's life is a late-night matter and, therefore, a late-morning matter. One of the hitmen broke through the doorway, blasting his shotgun. Cy grabbed his gun, but it was too late. The goon got him right in the chest with "fifty shotgun slugs." (The writer probably meant buckshot.) Later, at Evanston Hospital, Cy Tearney didn't need Dr. Bridegroom to tell him he would recover. Glenview chief of police J.V. Miller dropped by for a little chat with the injured man. Cy claimed that he knew who entered his bedroom. And the guys who entered Cy's bedroom knew Cy knew.

The next night, two men visited Evanston Hospital, concerned about the state of Tearney's life or death—more so his death. The visitors asked the elevator attendant to take them to Mr. Tearney's room. He referred the "friends" to the night superintendent of nurses. When they were told that orders were not to admit anyone to the room, the pair hurriedly left the hospital. The authorities were contacted. Lieutenant Lester Laird of the county highway police was sure the two men had intended to kill Tierney, the first attempt having failed. Lieutenant Laird wasn't the type to smack a young soldier on the steps of Evanston Hospital, but he did make a list of things to do. Wondering why Chief Miller hadn't notified the highway police of Tearney's bullet-ridden body, he put a call in. But he would have to wait for the answer, as the chief had an emergency fishing trip that very day. The next interview went to Al Tearney, Cy's brother and owner of the closed-down downtown speakeasy, who might have some answers.

That night, Cy Tearney's condition took a turn for the worse. Dr. Bridegroom gave him little chance for recovery. But like Don Corleone in *The Godfather*, Cy Tearney lived to see many more days. And just like the Corleone family in New York, the Garden of Allah closed down. It's unknown if the Tearney brothers moved their operations to Lake Tahoe.

What is known is that long after the Garden burned down, in yet another mysterious fire, a rumor persisted that the body of a young woman, perhaps a moll, had been found on the patio. Supposedly, the gangsters were trying to cover up her untimely death. The problem is that there never was a single iota of proof to this rumor. Admittedly, the lingering intrigue adds some decent suspense to the Lyons School property. Maybe some rumor got tumbled up with the original Garden of Allah in Los Angeles.

VILLA VENICE BOMBING[61]

In early October 1929, a bomb exploded under the Villa Venice's front porch, causing $5,000 worth of damage when it blew out the front wall. Since the Villa Venice was a summer resort, it had closed a few weeks earlier, but Mrs. Bouche was there that night alone, as her husband was visiting his Florida interests. The county highway police stated it was a consequence of the beer racketeers' war. The gangs were intruding into the suburbs.

On August 28, 1930, it was reported in the *Chicago Tribune*, "The Lake Avenue Tavern, Glenview, said to have enjoyed a lucrative trade since the air races began, was raided by prohibition agents yesterday. Charles Klein was arrested." Frank Engels couldn't have been too happy when "the raiders said they found beer and whiskey." Thanks to good old American capitalism, the "build it and they will come" attitude reigned along West Lake Avenue (now Chestnut). A few new bars like the Airfield Inn, Air-Port Bar-B-Que and the Airport Tavern greeted any guest to Curtiss Reynolds with a shot and a beer. The dry raiders didn't seem to want their beer and whiskey.

WRONG MOVE AT THE LAKE AVENUE TAVERN[62]

The night before Thanksgiving 1930, it was just past midnight, and Frank Engels was hanging out toward the back room of his bar, anxious to close. Jack Hackney's place on Harms had been held up a few weeks earlier, and only three nights earlier, there was a ruthless holdup at Henry Goetz's joint in Summit. Frank read in the *Tribune* that at one o'clock in the morning, eight thugs lined everyone up against the wall at Goetz's and went through the pockets and purses of the silent minority. James Mikus, a railroad detective, stumbled out of the john, saw the bandits and started shooting. The gang leader yelled to turn up the lights, but the stupe got confused and turned off the lights instead. Now, everyone was either shooting or shrieking. Frank liked to think his bartender friend Goetz ordered his Great Dane to sic the little punk, and the good dog obeyed orders like, well, like a Great Dane. The dog found the meanest, smallest, baby-faced gangster and took a good bite out of his leg. That sent the hoods scrambling out the front door, the gang leader limping, as well as Mikus, as he had been shot. But being a detective—even if only a railroad detective—he was determined to get these guys. He hobbled to his car to follow the slugs but lost them in the traffic (traffic at one thirty in the morning? In Summit?). Back at the Summit roadhouse, three college girls were on their way to the undertaker, and four bullet-ridden bodies were keeping the surgeons busy. Cops scoured the hospitals for dog-bitten, trigger-happy thugs who had caused this disaster for a lousy $200. Yeah, Frank Engels was ready to call it a night.

Russell Thompson Breezes In

Frank glanced at the clock: 12:05 p.m. The front door opened, ushering in a chilly breeze. So much for closing early. Giving the patron a second look, he realized it was Russell Thompson. In this business, Frank knew many people, and they were all friends, but not everyone was like Russell Thompson. People said he was café society, but you'd never know it by talking with him. You could just shoot the breeze with Russell. No airs. And fun. Even the customers perked up when he stopped by. This fellow bouncing in could barely contain himself with the news that his wife was at Evanston Hospital in childbirth. (Frank didn't know it at the time, but in nine months, forty-two-year-old Betty would be delivering their own surprise package.) Thompson took to a barstool, giving his chicken sandwich order to George Miller, the waiter. It was crazy, what happened next. Within minutes, the saloon went haywire.

Frank Engels was casually hanging by the side door, talking to Thompson, when two masked gunmen materialized, guns in hand, pointed at him. At the same time, two of the gang's buddies hurried through the front door. The icy cold these two sported was not from the winter chill. One of them yelled, "Stick 'em up. This is a holdup!" Russell Thompson, the joy boy on the barstool, still in his glee, a bit in his cups, thinking this was some kind of a joke, turned a bit too slow, laughed and, unfortunately, didn't stick 'em up fast enough for the rifle-shooting thug. The gunman didn't appreciate Thompson's humor, and in his anger, so antagonized, he flat-out, point-blank shot the father-to-be square in the chest. It was as though he was used to shooting people. Then, as if he had barely swatted a fly, the killer arrogantly stepped over Thompson's still warm body and aimed his smoking gun to force the waiter and Frank to the safe.

All things considered, Frank was pretty cool when he suggested they call a doctor. The murderer suggested Frank shut up. With the threat of his gun, he redirected Frank to the safe for the colossal haul of $125. As the gang finished lifting a few extra valuables from the terrified clientele left in the roadhouse, one of the thieves weighed in, "It's a murder here. We better get going." With that cerebral insight, they fled through the front door to a waiting car with only parking lights on and sped off into the night.

Phone calls were made. Russell Thompson's father hurried to Frank's Tavern and helped the Glenview Police organize a hunt for the killers. The highway police were sure there would be a quick resolution to this crime when they found the stock of a shotgun on the saloon floor. The bureau of identification at the Chicago Detective Bureau would research the fingerprints. Frank Engels gave a decent description of the murderer: five feet, eleven inches, 170 pounds, thin face with dark skin. He wore a dark coat and hat. Frank swore he could recognize him if he saw him again.

Months went by. Nothing occurred except funerals and births.

In the previous year, prior to this grisly murder, a series of bank thefts and house jewelry thefts had been exasperating the police from Lake Forest to the Gold Coast. One of those robberies was that of Mrs. William Hale Thompson, wife of the corrupt "Big Bill," mayor of Chicago—the same mayor who liked to drive a half day to Aptakisic for a homemade Sunday dinner. She told reporters that her robber "had a babyish face. He was good-looking." Thus, the Baby Face name was born for George Nelson, although his quick temper kept anyone close to him from using it. His birth name was Lester Gillis; his friends called him Jimmy. On February 14, 1931, eight people, including the famed Lester "Baby Face Nelson" Gillis, were arrested after a one-month stakeout. Two days later, the assistant state's attorney, Charles J. Miller, declared ten sensational bank and jewelry robberies had been solved. And that's not all. Baby Face Nelson could also be the killer of E. Russell Thompson at the Lake Street Tavern and the killer of that massacre in Summit. It wasn't only Big Bill Thompson who was taking a sigh of relief.

Witnesses were assembled and questioned. However, when they were interviewed by the authorities, memories suddenly went forgotten, and the Lake Avenue Tavern murder was never in the *Chicago Tribune* again in connection with the infamous Baby Face Nelson. The mayor's wife, her Chicago policeman protector-driver and others also failed to remember the youthful-looking thug. Memories get shady when a victim comes face to face with a murderer.

On July 9, 1931, Baby Face Nelson was sentenced to a year to life at the state prison in Joliet. He was convicted only of the Hillside Bank robbery and a home invasion. So much for the ten sensational jewel robberies. So much for E. Russell Thompson.

A Dumb Young One

Almost a year after Russell Thompson was shot through the chest at Frank Engels's place, an exciting development arose. On November 5, 1931, seventeen-year-old Edward Roehl was seized when police found him armed with a revolver and dumdum bullets (banned bullets that explode on impact) in front of the Abbot Avenue Apartments in Chicago. The police reported, "He and another youth were planning to rob a bank in Carthage, NY and escape on an airplane." Yes, the statement bears considerable disbelief.

Detectives Harry Schaff and Emil Boettcher entered the apartment with their guns drawn. The young adults in the apartment fought back, thinking the men were robbers. One of the detectives shot Clare Christensen in his right hip. The shooting calmed them down enough for the detectives to arrest Clare with his brother Albert; Albert's wife, Louis Bruneau; two other young men; and two young women. The prisoners were taken to the Sheffield Station and questioned by Captain Christensen. The next day, the two detectives were suddenly reduced to the rank of patrolmen. It appears they bungled the raid, unless the captain's comment is considered, as he "had nothing against the men adding that he might recommend them for extra compensation." It's possible Captain Christensen was a bit testy at how the arrested Christensens were treated. Talk about a shot in the hip.

In the meantime, various news reports announced that Edward Roehl confessed that it was he who shot and killed E. Russell Thompson during a holdup in the Lake Avenue Tavern in Glenview a year earlier. He was arraigned with two accomplices, Louis Bruneau, twenty-three, and Frank Tey, twenty-two, before the Morton Grove magistrate. The three of them were charged with murder and sent to the county jail. A *Journal Gazette* reporter talked to young Ed Roehl and wrote, "At the end of his youthful trail of escapades, a 17-year-old Edward Roehl sat in a cell calmly retelling how he had shot a man to death during a holdup of a roadhouse last Thanksgiving Eve."

A practice that is staggeringly illegal in today's norms but was perfectly acceptable, above board and bona fide on November 6, 1931, was the reenactment of the crime, as described in the *Journal Gazette*:

> *Policemen, reporters, and photographers trooped into the room of the Lake Avenue Tavern....In the midst of a crowd, managed by a detective, was an overgrown, sleepy-eyed youth, Edward Roehl, 17 years old, from Winnetka, former student of New Trier High School and the Missouri Military Academy of Mexico, Missouri. "Now, where were you standing when the shot was fired?" demanded Captain A.C. Christensen. The boy shuffled over to a table at the wall, his guard stepping awkwardly beside him. "Now let me get this straight," he said, labored, plucking his lips, "I was stiff on a pint of alcohol that night and I'm still kind of hazy in my mind. I was standing here covering the crowd with a shotgun. Mr. Thompson came in from the dining room or the bar. He made a fast move and the gun went off." The youth shoved his hat back and scratched his forehead reflectively. "I didn't see the rest," he said. "One of the gang grabbed my arm and hustled me out to the car. They knew I was wobbly. We hit east and took the first side road, north then east again. They must have ditched the gun in a creek by the Chicago River and the Northwestern Tracks because I didn't hear them [the guns] rattling on the floorboards after we crossed the bridge. The gang put me out at the hotel at 555 Surf Street where I was staying since they [his parents] put me out at home."*
>
> *"Then you didn't see them at the safe after Thompson fell?" asked Captain Christensen. The captain referred to Frank Tay, Louis Bruneau and Frank Fisher. "No, I don't know about the safe." The youth said, "Fisher took me to the car and drove."*
>
> *"You were double crossed on the split up," said the captain, "they got $125 from the safe." The crowd left the Lake Street Tavern and "with the prisoner pointing the way, the police party followed the getaway route and stopped at the creek beside the track, where the detectives poked in the reeds and stirred up the mud for twenty minutes in a vain search for the guns."*

Reporters then went to Roehl's mother's house and interviewed her. They were met by a mature, blonde, attractive woman, convinced her son was not a murderer. "He couldn't have done it," she said firmly. "He's a timid, overgrown boy. He was away at military school that night, or, no. He was at home and took Thanksgiving dinner with us. The police must have terrified him into admitting anything. You watch—we'll get a lawyer and prove him innocent."

The crowd continued their journey back to the jail. Two hours later, the young prisoner's "gray-haired, sprucely dressed stepfather" came to the jail. The *Tribune* reporters described his conversation with Edward Roehl:

> *The boy walked into the captain's office with his eyes on the ceiling. "Well, Eddie," he said, "in spite of everything in the past, I'm here to help you." "It's no use, Father," the boy replied, a trifle stagily, "You can do nothing for me now." "It's true then," the stepfather whispered, then continued in a harsher tone, "You've done your best in the last six years to kill your mother with your mischief. What can I tell her when I go home? I'm afraid this will finish it." Edward walked back to his cell rubbing his eyes. The stepfather briefly told his troubles to the captain—the boy's persistent truancy from school, his pilfering, his running up extravagant charge accounts and finally his flight from the military school two months after his parents paid $2,000 tuition to rid him of evil companions. "But I can't understand how he could become a killer. He grew up fast and ran with older fellows. He's always been a half yellow. I always thought him cowardly." "It's that kind that shoots quickly," the captain said. Bruneau, a pale ferret-faced youth, whom Capt. Christensen regarded as the leader of the gang, and Tay who had spent time in a San Francisco jail, insisted last…they had never been near the Lake Avenue Tavern.*

Six months after Edward Roehl confessed to shooting E. Russell Thompson at the Lake Street Tavern in Glenview; six months after he bragged about the cold-blooded murder, although he remembered few details; six months after he was charged with the murder although police found little evidence, Edward Roehl was *nolle prossed* on April 14, 1932. Two interesting "facts" brought about this prosecutor's formal entry, which simply indicated he would no longer prosecute a pending criminal charge. One is the acting first assistant state's attorney's discussion with Roehl's alienists (1932's word for psychiatrists), who found their patient "to be legally sane but suffering from hallucinations." "Since the state depended on Roehl's confession entirely for the prosecution, the case collapsed when he repudiated the statement."

The other "fact" was that Edward Roehl and his partner, Louis Bruneau, were also indicted for stealing seventy-five dollars from a restaurant on North State Street on October 27, 1931. This charge was also *nolle prossed* when the robbed cashier said she had been mistaken in her identification of Roehl. The four young men were set free, and another Glenview killing went unsolved.

MATT HOFFMAN'S SAD SWAN SONG[63]

Matt Hoffman was strong. He got strong when he was in the ice business and had to haul ice blocks up three-story flats and down into basements. He could pick up a barrel of beer like it was nothing. A half barrel weighed about 120 pounds plus the weight of the barrel. He liked carrying his own barrels. He loved checking up on his brew operations. He couldn't help it. He loved the whole business.

But by 1931, Matt had three young tots, a scared wife and a lush beer business. Matt was selling his beer to most Glenview joints, a few in Northfield and one or two in Morton Grove. He tried to stay out of Morton Grove. He sold his beer to family customers in Wilmette and Kenilworth, who were buying it by the case. These were the same people who promoted Prohibition because they didn't want booze in their backyards. Funny, they didn't mind the booze in their basements. Hypocrisy at its finest. But they had the money.

Matt sold his half barrels to Al and Fred Krueger's, across from North Shore Gardens. Another Krueger brother, Ernie, owned a joint by Glenview Road and Waukegan. Matt sold his beer to Dilg's Glen View House, Jingles by the airport and Frank Engels's place on Lake Street. He sold barrels at about fifty dollars but charged sixty dollars to the Elks Club in Evanston.

There were those who said Matt could be ruthless. Elmer Werhane, the milkman, was driving through Glenview when a young father stopped him and asked if the milkman could give his little boy a ride in his truck. This was no problem for Elmer, as he did not provide the kind of ride known by the gangster trade. The week wasn't over when the milkman saw the child's father again, who begged him to take an hour off for lunch at Frank Engels's place. Elmer, who could never afford lunch, was shocked by the next turn of events.

We were sitting there (right in the middle of the bar) and Matt Hoffman comes in the side door. "Oh, hello Frank" he says. Frank evidently owed him some money because, in those days, everybody trusted everybody. Well, he came in and Frank turned white! Matt was like Al Capone, "the big boy." "Frank," he says, "don't be scared. I just come to collect a little money." He no sooner said that then two of those Italian boys came in the front door. My heart just sunk.…You know how Al Capone had boys with him as bodyguards, Well, he [Matt] had four of them! If there was going to be a shooting, I would have been right in the middle of it. [Matt Hoffman then said,] "I didn't mean to scare you like that, just give the boys a little drink."

Ann Hoffman was scared. Andy Andersen was scared. Ann's brother Leo Schneider was scared. Matt never saw the writing on the wall. Yes, Matt knew Gross Point and Glenview like the back of his hand. But the best, the very best, the most supreme thing was that his wife, his sweetheart, this little lady who grew up with him, this wonderful honey of his, loved him and was on his side. All he knew was that he was the luckiest guy in the world.

He Put Her Through Hell

That hell was Roger Touhy, who continued to finagle his brewery possibilities; it seems he also explored other market potential, the best market potential being Matt Hoffman. In February 1931, Roger Touhy gave Matt Hoffman an ultimatum. Touhy wanted Matt's beer recipe. He also told Matt to quit selling his half barrels to anybody. In return, Matt could sell bottled beer north of Howard Street. Now, who was thinking Matt Hoffman was born yesterday? Or had two left feet? In an unfeigned, unreserved, stupidly unguarded, plain-spoken straightforwardness, Matt said to Roger Touhy, "Nothing doing. I'm the boss out here." And he was, but not for long.

So much for Roger Touhy and "share the wealth." So much for the "enough here for everybody" philosophy that he had spouted a few years earlier. Roger might have been a good egg about not wanting Capone in his territory. Capone, who had tried to bring prostitution to the northern suburbs. Altar boy Roger Touhy, bless his heart, kept the holy land west of Harlem safe for schoolboys and husbands. He paid off-duty cops $100 a week to drive his bootlegger trucks, and politicians were satisfied with a barrel of his quality brand of beer every couple of months. The trouble was, now he wanted Matt's customers, and Matt was happy carrying his own barrels, thank you.

Roger bullied anybody who bugged him. He was good at it and becoming better every day. He had to keep Capone out, especially since Moran had moved his properties up by Wisconsin. Matt Hoffman was just another rival and needed to be gone. Roger needed to intimidate Matt Hoffman, so he drove up and down Matt's street late at night looking for him, provoking him. Ann saw the bully out her window. After her husband refused to give in, Touhy would pull into the family driveway and open his car door, staring at the windows silently, with his foot on the gas pedal. Ann would call her brother Leo, begging him to go find Matt and tell him not to come home, as these monsters were waiting for him. She used to call Charlie Bohn too. He "couldn't say how many times Ann used to call me. They were riding up and down the road looking for him. Waiting for him to come home, I guess. I used to go out and see if I could find him and tell him not to go home. They were after him for at least six months before they got him."

Charlie Bohn told another chilling story about those few months before Matt Hoffman was killed. "We came from Wheeling one time with a load of bottles. We were coming down Lehigh, and I said, 'Matt, they're behind us. They're going to get us.' He had a big old Buick, and he shot across the railroad tracks by Rugen's Tavern and ran in. They never came in."

One night, Ann watched in horror as Touhy's gang pulled into their yard and threatened her husband. They demanded that he get out and not interfere with their business.

That summer of 1931, Matt Hoffman brought his new friend Jake Schreiber to Jack Hackney's Harms Road blind pig. Matt told Hackney that if Schreiber ever wanted a couple of barrels, Hackney should call Matt, no matter what time it was. Matt kept half barrels of beer in his basement, and he could easily throw a couple in his car and get them to Jack's in a matter of minutes.

A New Lawn

It was hot on July 30, 1931. Jack Hackney glanced out his window at the full moon, glad that he and Bebe had finally gotten their new lawn planted. It was about time. He was hoping that little wire fence would keep people off the fresh grass and give it a chance to grow. The door opened, and Jake Schreiber, Matt's new friend, stalked in. Jack was all ready to smile and say hello to him when suddenly Jake Schreiber's gun targeted itself on Jack's handsome forehead. Matt's new friend ordered Jack to take a nice deep breath, collect his composure and call his beer supplier buddy.

It was 10:30 p.m., and a mile away, Matt and Ann Hoffman were almost asleep. Hearing the phone ring, Ann wearily answered it and told her husband it was important he talk to Jack Hackney. Important indeed because back at the bar, it must have seemed to Jack that the gun against his head felt like a cannon. Jack did his best to keep his wits, calmly telling his friend that Jake Schreiber had stopped by and needed two half barrels of beer. Pronto.

Matt Hoffman portrait. *Courtesy George R. Pinkowski Jr.*

As his three children slept, Matt threw his pants on over his pajama bottoms. He didn't even bother putting on a shirt and ran out of the house in his undershirt and bedroom slippers. Back on Harms Road, to Jack's immense relief, Jake withdrew the gun and left the bar, telling Jack that when Matt rolled in with the beer, Matt should wait for him.

Not long after the phone call, Matt pulled into Jack's yard and got out of the car but could see some suspicious-looking people inside the doorway at Hackney's. Before they even came out the door, Matt tore off in the dark. He knew they were after him. What he didn't see was the short wire fence on the new lawn, and down he went. By that time, those bastards were there, and *bang, bang, bang*!

Not an hour later, Jack Hackney was explaining to the police, "Along about 11:00, or maybe a little later a car comes into my yard. Then about ten minutes more, I heard somebody yelling, 'Help, Jack.' I was afraid to go out, and there was some more noise. I didn't hear any shots fired. Pretty soon, two cars drove away, and I called the police to tell them I thought Matt had been kidnapped." The police chief and the county highway force investigated the scene outside the roadhouse and found two half barrels of beer and two shells from a .32-caliber pistol surrounding a pool of blood, but no Matt Hoffman.

Then There Was Leo

The night Matt was shot, Leo Schneider, Matt's partner and brother-in-law, went to the ice cream stand where his girlfriend worked. As Elsie told it, he was as white as a sheet. When she asked him if he was sick, he told her about Matt. Leo hung out in the back of the stand while she continued working. Both noticed a strange car with "characters" seeming to case the place. Leo fled into the basement. Finally, when the stand closed, Leo headed to Ann's and slept at her house because she was so afraid. Before the night was over, though, the hoods had found him and carted him up to the state line of Wisconsin, where they beat him up. Elsie said that he had the scars from whip lashes on his back until the day he died, although he never said a word about it. They didn't kill him because he convinced them he didn't know the real name of the Dutchman and he didn't know how to make the beer. They just whipped him and let him go in the middle of nowhere. He called his brother Pete, who rescued him and got him back home. Once again, the sons of Elsie and Leo commented on their parents' lucky break, or else the boys would not have been born to hear the story.

Who Done It?

The next day, a couple of farmers' sons, Roman Raupp and Clarence Weidner, were walking through a cornfield near Aptakisic when they saw a man sleeping. The boys continued on their way. Hours later, on their return trip, they saw the same body in the same position, and this time, they realized it was probably a dead man. The boys contacted the authorities. Deputy Sheriff John DeSchmidt, who had known Matt, identified the poor dead thirty-two-year-old. Matt Hoffman's car was found in Bensenville. Suburban newspapers went back and forth over which band of bandits had caused this tragedy. The papers in DeKalb believed "the slayers were Wisconsin men who hoped to take over Hoffman's territory." Closer to home, the Glenview police focused their investigation on Capone's takeover of the Glenview district.

After the gang-style murder, Jack Hackney was missing. Furthermore, Jake Schreiber, Matt's new friend, the one who held the gun to Jack Hackney's head, was also missing. Andy Andersen was so scared for his life that he jumped a train and got off in Calamus, Iowa. His Irish twins didn't hear from him for another twenty years.

A minor sigh of relief came over Glenview when it was reported that Jack Hackney was being protected by the Glenview police after two unidentified hoodlums stopped by his place the Saturday after Matt's disappearance, threatening him "to keep his mouth shut or go the same way as Hoffman." Years later, Mary Welsh, Jack Hackney's niece, disclosed that the threats were so imminent that Frank Engels kept Jack Hackney hidden for weeks.

It's not clear if Glenview police chief Miller was deaf, blind, dumb or lying when he said the syndicate was "laying off" Glenview since the killing of Russell Thompson nine months earlier, while at the same time keeping their eye on Matt Hoffman's activities. After that puzzling statement, considering there had been two ruthless murders in the village in less than a year, the police chief then ordered a preemptive strike against gang warfare by "declaring police guards and early closing of all roadhouses until the trouble blows over to avoid further disturbances." Seeing that Miller had suddenly gone on a fishing trip two years earlier during the shooting at the Garden of Allah, there doesn't seem to be any surprise that this was another murder never solved.

The chief might have been right. A few days later, there was a "disturbance" in Wilmette. Adolph Dumont, thirty-eight, was driving along Central Avenue, close to his home, when he noticed several unsavory-looking characters in a large blue motorcar following him. Being the sophisticated and respectable North Shore realtor that he was and probably scared witless, he made tracks to the police station. But the big blue sedan masterfully brought its prey to the curb and forced Dumont out of his car to "take him for a ride" in their car. When he resisted their efforts, they shot him, the bullet shattering his upper arm at the shoulder. At Evanston Hospital, he was able to talk to the police before dying from the loss of blood.

The police believed this assault was yet another exhortation from the crime world. The Wilmette police further disclosed that A.J. Dumont feigned total ignorance of the reason for this attack, except maybe robbery, as he did tend to carry large amounts of cash. The police probably listened cynically and pointed out that the shooters neglected to take his diamond-studded watch or $600. Additional analysis produced Dumont's police records dating back to 1903, the first being a larceny that yielded a three-year sentence at the Pontiac reformatory. He had fourteen other arrests for pickpocketing and burglary, which contributed to fines and short prison terms at Bridewell. Quite the man about town, that jaunty Mr. Dumont. Police also revealed that Dumont had interests in two cafés, the Walton

Club in Morton Grove and one in Chicago. Yet even in death, it's the woman behind the man who makes the man. Thanks to testimony given by Mrs. Dumont, it was determined that not only did her husband not have any enemies, but he also didn't have any connections with gangsters, bootleggers or any other sordid types. There was no Walton Club, at least not any that poor, dear departed Mr. Dumont had anything to do with. The inquest verdict was thus announced, "murder by persons unknown."

It's fishy that the police didn't let on that Teddy Newberry owned the Walton clubs. Newberry, it just so happens, was walking down Clark Street with Bugs Moran the morning of the St. Valentine's Day Massacre when the two decided to go for coffee instead of attending what they thought was a police raid at SMC Cartage. After that, Newberry defected to the Capone gang. And after that, Capone gave him the whole North Side in August 1930. By this time, Moran had gotten the message, given up the gang wars and moved his operations to Lake County, Illinois, and southern Wisconsin.

The Morton Grove Walton Club was down the street from a joint called the Club Morton, which was owned by Roger Touhy's good buddy and brewing partner Matt Kolb. They sold their beer in Morton Grove and all points west of Harlem Avenue. With Matt Hoffman gone, Touhy imagined more control. Two months later, on October 18, 1930, two men stepped into the Club Morton. Kolb extended his hand, and like during the O'Banion murder, one of the thugs held tight on his arm while the other one pumped him full of bullets. And just like the O'Banion murder, one thug came back and shot him again. Waukegan Road taverns were turning into killing fields.

Charlie Bohn talked about one time he had seen Roger Touhy after Matt Hoffman was shot. He said it was in a tavern in Morton Grove.

> He was a pretty rough boy. A guy in the tavern was doing the same thing. He was selling beer too. Roger came walking in around 12:30 with his four "boys." He took his revolver out and hit this guy right thru the mouth. He broke out all his teeth in front. He said, "I told you, you SOB, not to make any beer and sell it. I don't want to see you here when I come back in a half-hour." That was it, and they walked out.

So much for being an altar boy.

Jack Hackney might have had some protection from the police, but nobody saw him for months. He was never the same after that. He became a recluse.

He quietly passed away in 1939, and a few months later, his pretty wife followed him in death. Hackney's on Harms was passed on to Jim Masterson and his new wife, Kitz, for a dollar.

Roger Touhy got a good break when Capone was sentenced to eleven years in prison on a tax evasion charge in 1931. In the end, Capone would have the last laugh. Capone framed Touhy for the Jake Factor kidnapping (held in a house on Fir and Elm Streets). Touhy was arrested and tried with the Capone gang. False testimony was given, and Touhy was sentenced to ninety-nine years at Stateville. Touhy was out of the picture.

ATTENTION ALL CARS, ATTENTION ALL CARS, BE ON ALERT[64]

On November 27, 1934, the Glenview State Bank received a call from the FBI to be on the alert for notorious bank robbers; Dillinger and his boys had been seen in the area. The bank doors were kept locked that day, and only known customers were allowed in. This was a good idea, since the FBI had a shootout with the gang at Dundee Road and Northwest Highway that day and shot Baby Face Nelson after he blasted two federal agents. A very shot-up Baby Face Nelson managed to escape from the scene, but the next morning, his body was found near a cemetery in Niles Center (now Skokie).

In 1967, federal files became available to the public with the Freedom of Information Act. It wasn't until the 1980s that the FBI began releasing occasional files on its "war on crimes" major cases. The exhaustive research of Bryan Burrough, author of *Public Enemies*, published in 2004, finally uncovered the reality of this horrible crime, unfortunately long past the time anyone could be held accountable. Stanton J. Randall, a member of the Nelson gang and one of the gunmen at the Lake Street Tavern, was interviewed by the FBI in 1934. Jimmy "Baby Face Nelson" Gillis was indeed the killer in the brazen murder of E. Russell Thompson in front of his friend Frank Engels. The Nelson gang members were also the killers of the three women in the Summit, Illinois roadhouse murders.

Baby Face Nelson, the man never tried for shooting Edwin Russell Thompson at the Lake Avenue Tavern on Thanksgiving Eve 1930, was described by a Chicago assistant attorney as "a tough little s--t." After the death of John Dillinger, Nelson, who graduated to Public Enemy #1, was being followed by special agent Herman Hollis and Inspector Samuel

Lester Gillis, aka "Baby Face Nelson." *Courtesy Dave Alexander, Legends of America.*

Cowley, who were ordered by the U.S. Justice Department to "shoot first and ask questions later." After receiving news that Nelson was in Wisconsin, the agents spotted him, his wife and gangster pal John Paul Chase driving toward Chicago on Northwest Highway in Barrington. But ten minutes earlier, another set of agents had identified that his car was stolen and started chasing Nelson. The maniac, Nelson, made a U-turn so he could pursue them, shooting the whole time. When the agents noticed Nelson was no longer behind them, they speeded off to their headquarters, admitting, "This isn't going to look too good. We're federal officers. Weren't we supposed to be chasing them?"

A few miles east, in front of three gas stations, an off-duty cop and more than thirty witnesses, Nelson realized that another car was following him. Hollis was driving the Hudson while Cowley fired his tommy gun at the speeding Ford V-8, forcing Nelson's car off the road when his engine was hit. Still attempting to outrun the cops, Nelson turned into a side road when his vehicle petered out. Nelson and Chase spilled out of their car to finish the gunfight while his wife ran into the field to lay low. Seconds later, agent Cowley shot Nelson near his stomach, piercing his liver and pancreas with a bullet that went right through his back. Never one to give an inch or back down from a fight, Nelson tried holding his bleeding guts together with one hand and stepped out in front of the barrage of bullets, shooting a .351 rapid-fire shotgun. He plugged both agents full of holes. In all their wounded gall and arrogance, the gangsters got their guns from the Nelson car, put them in the agents' car and started driving off. Nelson's wife ran out from the field and jumped in the car. They drove to a safe house in Wilmette near 17th Street and Walnut, where Nelson died. An unidentified man from the safe house carried his body out of the house with his poor wife at his side. She cradled his naked body, covered with a Navajo blanket, and they laid him near a cemetery near Harms Road in Skokie. The twenty-five-year-old has the distinction of being the only person to kill three FBI agents.

As 1928 was winding down,[65] the public was tiring of the drinking restrictions, obvious in the nature of *Chicago Tribune* articles such as "Tavern Coming Back Into Its Own," "Dry Era Knocks Joy from Dining, Rector Asserts," "U.S. Prohibition Farce to British Woman Official," "Sheriff Explains: If Citizens Would Take More Interest, Conditions Would Be Better" and, finally, "Enjoying a Nip No Crime, Says Senator Blease."

CHAPTER 6

HAPPY DAYS ARE HERE AGAIN

T he Roaring Twenties slowly deflated into the Great Depression as a new decade began.[66] Across the plains of the United States, lack of rain, risky bank strategies and a grain surplus caused prices to fall and jobs to vanish. Glenview made it through the Depression, mainly because of its small farms, headquarters of truck farming operations and its many nurseries. Since there was little manufacturing, fewer people lost jobs. Thanks to the conservative nature of the Glenview State Bank, it fared well, unlike the 744 banks that failed in the first ten months of the worst economic tragedy the United States has ever known. Glenview's more than thirty bars, saloons, inns and roadhouses certainly helped weather the financial crunch. Bartenders were happy to continue extending their services, aiding Depression strugglers for anyone who cared to stop in for a pop.

Rugen Stores[67] extended credit upon credit to its loyal customers. Neighbors who were short on cash could always count on Betty Engels at the Lake Avenue Tavern, who acted as a neighborhood pawnbroker, an indelicate word for a woman sincerely concerned about her friends. Betty would borrow the have-not's necklace, ring or any piece of jewelry and lend the needed money to help, kind of like a relative's advance. Her secret hiding place for the

Rugen Stores ad. *From the Glenview View, December 18, 1936.*

farmers' valuables was a hidden drawer behind an upstairs radiator. Years later, two of her grandchildren were roughhousing and fell on top of the radiator, and like magic, all sorts of bracelets, rings and things spilled out over the floor.

President Hoover's meager ideas and scorn of government intervention weren't getting food into hungry mouths for most of the country. The invisible hand theory was quickly generating invisible jobs.

"Roosevelt Sweeps All U.S."[68]

Franklin Roosevelt would change all that as he campaigned for a New Deal, claiming, "Ours must be a party that extends the greatest good to the greatest number of our citizens." The starving Americans ate it up, and it was about time. All over America, crowds sang his theme song, "Happy Days Are Here Again." He beat incumbent president Herbert Hoover, who won only six northeastern states, in a landslide. FDR was the first Democrat in eighty years to win an outright majority in popular and electoral votes, with an enormous count of 472 to 59.

The new president barely made it to bed that first night of his inauguration, he was so anxious to get America moving again. The first thing he did was to establish a moratorium on banks. For his second move, he said to Congress, "I think it's time the country did something about beer." Cheering and applause boomed through the galleries with the passage of the Cullen-Harrison Act, which legalized the sale of 3.2 beer. It's well known that more than cheers broke out that day, especially from the president. That night, "a festooned truck, escorted by a police detail, pulled up to the White House delivering two crates of the city's new brew. President Roosevelt, the first real beer is yours. Crowds braved the midnight rain, cheering at the gates." A few months later, when the news came at 8:30 p.m. on December 4, 1933, that Utah had ratified the Twenty-First Amendment, FDR was said to have stayed up until midnight so he could be the first to legally celebrate with his favorite martini.

Prohibition ultimately failed because at least half the adult population wanted to carry on drinking. Policing of the Volstead Act was riddled with contradictions, biases and corruption, and the lack of a specific ban on consumption hopelessly muddied the legal waters. To be honest, while there was a desire to curb the antisocial effects and the moral degradation of drinking, there was no national will to stop the act of drinking itself.

President Franklin D. Roosevelt signing one of his many bills. *Courtesy RBM Vintage Images/ Alamy Stock Photo.*

Prohibition had transformed America's drinking habits, although not in the way the ASL had hoped. Drinking did decrease for a time, and the man caves that allowed males to stand around with their shot and a beer, spitting, throwing up and passing out on the floors, were gone. Women could go to bars without risking a bad reputation. Drinking was no longer the demon that ruined lives, instead becoming normalized and accepted. In fact, the very word *saloon* was retired as more couples and families sought out the pleasure of a bar for a good meal, dancing and a cocktail or two. Another welcome influence with the repeal of Prohibition was that it was harder, not easier, to get a drink. Regulations came into effect controlling closing hours, age limits and Sunday Blue Laws.

In Illinois, the State Department and the Liquor License Control Commission decided to go all out in a drive to enforce liquor licenses. Director K.L. Ames proclaimed, "The department must protect the citizen who observes the law, and the only way this can be done is by rigid enforcement impartial and fair." Glenview instituted liquor laws that included retail bar licenses to six Class A taverns, four Class B and 3 Class C. That was less than half of the bars, taverns, resorts and roadhouses in Glenview at that

Workmen unload crates of beer stacked at a New York brewery shortly after the repeal of Prohibition. *Courtesy Keystone/Staff/Getty Images.*

time. They could stay in business until they retired or closed down. The first violation pulled the plug on Chateau Gardens on Waukegan Road, near Winnetka Avenue, for serving minors from the Civilian Conservation Corps. Thanks to these limits, Glenview saloon owners could finally breathe a sigh of relief and come out of the closet.[69] Frank Engels was the first to apply for the new village liquor license at the surprisingly affordable fifteen dollars a year. Meier's Tavern no longer had to hide behind its pony rink, and the Willow Inn quit pretending it was a gun club.

MATTY'S WAYSIDE INN[70]

In 1931, at the subtly named Blind Pig, Matty and Erna Fegers served martinis and beers for a dime from the living room of the old Lockman family farmhouse. Soon they added four tables and a six-stool bar, though they were sometimes without a phone and occasionally had no power. The Fegerses served a prime rib dinner for $1.15. When Prohibition ended, they came out of the closet with a new name, Matty's Wayside Inn, when

Matty's Wayside Inn. *From* Glenview, the First Centennial.

Bar in Matty's Wayside Inn. *From* Glenview, the First Centennial.

A meeting of 1940s area bartenders, including John Dilg, Frank Meier, Herb Rugen and Frank Engels. *Courtesy Gus Pappas, Meier's Tavern.*

they received their liquor license: No. 6. In the next twenty years, Matty's continued to add various dining rooms and country views to a garden. Matty and Erna retired to let Matty Jr. take over, telling him, "Serve good food, and keep the place clean." Matty's Wayside Inn was a favorite Glenview icon until it burned down in October 2009, to the grief of many.

The Glen View House and the Blue Heron stocked their cellars again. Hackney's ignored its past to create what would become Glenview's favorite meeting place. Rugen's Tavern, another staple, was crowded, primarily due to its proximity to the train station. As their drinking business dried up, the gangs put more of their considerable weight into gambling operations, but that is another book.

Achieving the most severe penalty[71] up to this day, Al Capone was sentenced to eleven years in prison on October 17, 1931, for tax evasion. He arranged to bribe the jury, but the judge pulled a switcharoo at the last minute and traded the bribed jury for a jury chosen for another, more benign case. His conviction secured, Capone's first three years were spent "languishing" in an Atlanta penitentiary, listening to radio serials with his well-tipped guards in his carpeted cell, flush with nearby family and constant visitors. Al Capone could afford to tip the guards with the $62 million he had amassed. Tired of his antics, the head of federal prisons had him transferred to Alcatraz.

Repeal Day at Sloppy Joe's Bar in downtown Chicago. *Courtesy Everett Collection Historical/ Alamy Stock Photo.*

When he couldn't bribe the guards or manipulate the warden, Capone said, "It looks like Alcatraz has got me licked." When he was released from prison in November 1939, syphilis had left him with the mind of a twelve-year-old.

Barely surviving the St. Valentine's Day Massacre[72] had Bugs Moran scared. By May 1930, he had moved his liquor operations toward Wisconsin. Besides his high-scale bootlegging and gambling operations, his main moneymaking thrust had moved from the drinking business to exhorting the dry-cleaning unions, with his well-known bullying and killing tactics. There is some evidence that the Glenview Cleaners and Dryers was associated with him in 1926–27. During this short time, the cleaners advertised on the front page of the Glenview phone book. Suddenly, the small business disappeared, along with the man who ran the company. Moran was a reactionary, more interested in gunning down his enemies like a stupid streetfighter. By the 1940s, he had moved to Ohio and become a two-bit hustler, squandering the money he had made. He was jailed for robbing a bank messenger of $10,000, released after ten years and quickly jailed again. He spent most of his time in the prison hospital, dying of lung cancer on February 25, 1957, worth $100. He was buried in the prison cemetery.

Roger Touhy, the real con man[73] who held court over the Glenview saloons, was dealt the most ironic blow. Capone might have been in jail, but his people were strong on holding grudges. Touhy had a good relationship with Chicago mayor Anton Cermak. Touhy had been adept at keeping Capone's brothels out of Des Plaines, and Cermak's plan to clean up Chicago was to have Touhy's nonviolent gang "run the city." Promised the whole bootlegging operation of Chicago, Touhy started shooting at Capone's people in Chicago. Capone's gang returned fire in the suburbs. Capone kidnapped Touhy's partner Matt Kolb, extorting $50,000 for his return, and continued terrorizing Kolb's forty bars, clubs and resorts. Kolb was finally assassinated in his own Morton Club in Morton Grove on October 18, 1931. Touhy was also hustling unions during this time as he made his way into the Capone fortunes. In 1933, Jake Factor, as in the cosmetic fortune Factor, disappeared. Capone's Outfit finagled a kidnapping, making it look like it was Touhy's work. As a little-known fact, Factor was supposedly held in a

A 1933 photo of members of Roger Touhy's gang. Touhy is on the far left. *Courtesy Everett Collection Inc./Alamy Stock Photo.*

house on Fir Street in Glenview. The Outfit's plan worked.[74] Touhy was framed and sentenced to jail for ninety-nine years. That was the end of his gang. But the actual death knell of the gangs' liquor pursuits was the Twenty-First Amendment.

CAMPING IN THE WOODS ACROSS FROM HACKNEY'S[75]

If one of FDR's first and most popular programs wasn't opening bars, then surely it was the Civilian Conservation Corps. The CCC was enacted so quickly that the first recruit enlisted within two days of the president's act being signed. At a time when unemployment was 25 percent, the idea was to restore morale by recruiting unmarried, unemployed young male Americans and putting them to work with projects to clean up the environment and benefit the family budget. The young men would become self-reliant and economically independent. All this progress was a bargain for the government and a boon for the men at thirty dollars a month. One of the largest of the country's projects started out at Willow Road and Skokie Valley Road. When the owner realized some of the camp was on his property, he asked the government for rent. Camp Skokie Valley quickly found a new headquarters in Glenview, across from Hackney's on Harms. A total of 822 young adult men from poor families now had a purpose: to turn the Skokie marsh into an area of user-friendly lagoons.

And not a moment too soon. The Skokie marshes were the last vestiges of Chicago swamps that gave Chicago its name one hundred years earlier. Every time there was a spring deluge, the bogs caused flooding in basements near Willow Road and as far away as Glencoe and Winnetka. In the fall,

Civilian Conservation Corps center on Harms Road in Glenview. *Glenview History Center.*

peat fires erupted spontaneously, with some of the flames reaching eight feet high and three feet wide. The colossal flames would calm down after a few minutes, but the peat continued to burn for weeks, causing nearby neighbors to close their windows to the smoke and grime. Another problem was the Alfred Hitchcock–type clouds of mosquitos flying from the marshes to the lakefront, forcing people out of their gardens and into their homes. These had been sufferable nuisances since the beginning of the towns, and now the CCC boys were going to clean it all up. And they did it all without bulldozers, evacuating machines and other modern conveniences.

Major R.T. McCarron of the Sixth Infantry was the boss at Camp Skokie Valley (also called Camp Glenview), run by the War Department. The strategy was to handle the recruits in a similar way to armed forces training, minus the military labels like platoon and first sergeant. That meant no guns or drills. The boys lived in military-style barracks; performed group calisthenics, morning roll call and raising of the flag; ate in a mess hall; and stood at attention at the lowering of the flag in the evening. The army administrators paid, fed, housed, clothed, doctored and disciplined the men and managed the financial details, automatically sending home their twenty-five-dollar-a-month salary. The army personnel did not go into the fields with them. There, they worked under the supervision of the Cook County Forest Preserve staff.

Many of the new arrivals were just pitiful looking, thin and hollow-eyed. Some didn't have shirts. Others practically had no clothes. Others were well-dressed college students, high school grads, clerks, surveyors, chauffeurs, truck drivers, cooks and even a few young businessmen. Some were pretty good carpenters. The 289,000 men employed from coast to coast of this republic were busy ditching, draining and digging without using bulldozers or evacuating machines. According to the major, "Professional contractors don't turn out better work than these kids. The work is not Pollyanna, but it is respectable, productive, and cheerful." In no time, these "Depression victims" had tanned up and fleshed up in a forest setting of oaks and poplars. Three times a day, they had a good meal, typically beef stew with vegetables, bread and butter, chocolate pudding and iced tea. They were up at six o'clock, at work at eight, lights out at ten. "They get a fine example all the way—in big things and little from the finest gentlemen on earth. By that, I mean American regular army officers."

In this two-year project, the men created eight lagoons, three dams and six-foot-high dykes, reclaiming the area's forests. When they weren't doing their forty hours of digging through mud, their pastimes included listening to the radio and reading from the company library. Friends in nearby towns drove over with books and magazines. They watched movies two times a week and played ballgames against Fort Sheridan and other nearby towns. Proud Major McCarron thought these kids were better than any professional contractor and said, "I didn't vote for Franklin Roosevelt—I was scared—but when I left our Skokie camp, I said to myself, God bless the president of the United States."

Glenview welcomed the boys from the camp. How could they not? They spent their little bit of money at movie theaters, skating rinks and hamburger joints. Jim Masterson of Hackney's on Harms remembered that a good share of his good customers came from the CCC camp across the street. Masterson wasn't the only welcoming wagon from Glenview. According to the *Chicago Tribune*, "The monthly grocery and meat bill for the camp is $25,000, of which $20,000 is spent with the local merchants.

GLENVIEW STATE BANK FIRST IN COOK COUNTY TO BE 100 PERCENT LIQUID: BORROWERS PAID IN FULL[76]

During the financial tempest of the Depression, the Rugen family ran one of the few banks that didn't fail. Because of conservative supervision and true concern for their customers, this youngest bank in Cook County was the first to become fully liquid. It closed only one time, and that was when FDR's Bank Moratorium forced all banks to close on the new president's second day in office. He wasn't fooling around.

Glenview State Bank (GSB) was notified that $60,000 in capital was required before it could reopen. The officers went to work and raised the needed funds the best way they knew how: close relationships with friends, farmers and Glenview businesses that helped start this business only thirteen years earlier sprang into action. Unfortunately, founder Charlie Rugen died in 1929, but his banking practices lived on through village president E. Crebert Burnham and bank president Bill Smeal. The bank officers offered some of their friendlier depositors 10 percent interest if they would exchange their deposits for unsubordinated debt. To these heroes, that meant that if the bank filed bankruptcy, the friends got paid last and probably not at all. This was gutsy for a small-town bank, especially considering the prime rate was only 1½ percent. This risky venture, in the middle of the Depression, was reminiscent of *It's a Wonderful Life*. Like George Bailey, the Glenview businessmen, farmers and friends wanted—needed—the bank to open, and their trust was the evidence. Newspapers and honorees talked about commitment and perseverance; hogwash. It was pure Glenview neighborliness.

Twenty-two days after the forced closing, the state auditor brought his accounting books and pencils to Glenview and certified this little, youngest

Glenview State Bank. Always welcoming and generous with financial advice. *From the* Glenview View, *December 18, 1936.*

bank in northern Cook County to be in "first class condition." At 10:00 a.m. the next day, the bank opened to its unwavering supporters. When the cashiers finished counting the first day's cash deposits, GSB was $20,000 more prosperous. Glenview State Bank set an enviable record that few other banks in the country could equal.

Three and a half years later, the small-town bank that had lived out of a safe in the back of Rugen Stores less than fifteen years earlier was 100 percent liquid. Payback came quick in 1935, when on January 16, a 10 percent payment went to the loyal, if not lifesaving, depositors. Less than five months later, a 15 percent payment was made, followed by 25 percent on December 23. On May 1, 1936, another 15 percent was paid, and finally, on September 9, the final payment of 35 percent was made. Deposits grew so fast that they totaled more than twice as much as three and half years earlier. In the humble beauty of this small town, success continued on a handshake, prudence and loyalty.

SECOND TERM: "ROOSEVELT WINS; LANDSLIDE!"

By the end of his first term, President Roosevelt had instated the Social Security Act, Works Progress Administration and significant tax revision that opponents called the "soak-the-rich" tax that raised taxes on wealthy people and corporations.

The 1936 campaign was vicious. The Republican platform began, "America is in peril. The welfare of American men and women and the future of our youth are at stake. We dedicate ourselves to...political liberty...individual opportunity and character as free citizens, which today, for the first time, are threatened by government itself. For three long years the New Deal Administration has dishonored American tradition and flagrantly betrayed the pledges upon which the Democratic Party sought and received public support." In answer, Roosevelt proclaimed, "This generation of Americans has a rendezvous with destiny." Furthermore, he continued, "In this world of ours in the other lands, there are some people who, in times past have lived and fought for freedom, and seem to have grown too weary to carry on the fight. They have sold their heritage of freedom for the illusion of a living. They have yielded their democracy.… We are fighting to save a great and precious form of government for ourselves and for the world."

In the end, FDR won the largest contested victory in history when he beat Kansas governor Alf Landon. Roosevelt took every state in the Union except Maine and Vermont, with 523 electoral votes to Landon's 8. The Democrats gained twelve seats in the House and seven in the Senate.

Obviously, the show would go on, as did bars, saloons, nightclubs, watering holes, gin mills, beer gardens, lounges and roadhouses.

GLENVIEW BOONDOGGLE: THE WORKS PROGRESS ADMINISTRATION[77]

Just before Mother's Day, on May 6, 1935, Roosevelt established the Works Progress Administration. Critics whined that he was on the road to fascism or, worse, communism. Glenview locals grumbled about FDR ruining the country, despite his WPA policy committed to finding a job for the average citizen, offering dignity instead of suffering from being on the dole. The idea of rebuilding the country became more influential in 1939, when almost one-fifth of Americans needed to get back to work. The WPA evolved around a plan for projects if town officials would provide 20 percent of the money and 20 percent of the workforce.

The boondoggle that presented itself to the conservative leaders of Glenview in 1938 was the "socialist" project to finish Roosevelt Park and construct a pool for the community. The dream began long before the pool was built with an idea from Louis Cole, a landscape architect who grew up in Glenview. As explained by his daughter, Dorothy, "My father had a dream that what this town needed was some good public parks." He appealed to Carl Ladendorf and Edwin Rugen, and in 1927, the Glenview Park District was formed. Between the two men, they served eight terms and a total of fifty-one years. Other Park District officials at the time were George Fiske, Harold Cunliff and Edward Ganter, who helped develop Jackman Park, then Sleepy Hollow Park. What was needed, though, was an activity park. Among other things, Glenview citizens were skating in the winter and playing baseball in the summer.

Glenview Days, 1948. The first Glenview Days was celebrated in 1917 with the dedication of the Glenview Bear Fountain. As the years went on, the decorated cars, even by outside businesses, added to the length of the parade, probably due to prizes such as the best organization float, best industrial representation and best pleasure car. The parade traveled to Morton Grove, Niles Center, Niles and Northbrook. *Glenview History Center.*

After some maneuvering, Roosevelt Park was birthed on the combined property of one of Glenview's two original settlers, Henry Maynard's farmland, and Swain Nelson's nursery. The Park District also received its original garage and office building at 2320 Glenview Road from Swain. In 1932, the first paid director of parks, Louis Cole, designed the park with a pool, and Henry Maynard Jr. designed the fieldhouse at Roosevelt Park. His architectural plans are still displayed at the Park District Building.

Twenty-five years of Glenview Days had instilled in Glenview citizens the desire to binge on fun while raising money. Glenview was able to supply $5,000 toward the project, although workers had to be bussed in. "The Beach Away from the Lake" opened on July 4, 1940, and, for generations, provided Glenview kids with swimming lessons, entertainment, relaxation and opportunities for all ages. Roosevelt Pool

Roosevelt Park aerial view, including tennis courts (*upper left*), a round pool and four softball fields. Trees shield the tots' playground. *From* Glenview, the First Centennial.

became a historical monument, both in its unique design and structure. Out of 805 WPA swimming pools, today it is one of the only WPA pools in Illinois still running.

THE COMMUNITY HOUSE[78]

Glenview's first community center was a midwestern beauty with an open beamed ceiling and a stone fireplace. The large main room was used for all types of classes, including ballet and other dance programs. There were also arts and crafts and social gatherings held in that space. The district stopped using it in the late '70s after it acquired the old Rugen School and turned it into a community center. There was also a program space on the opposite side of the main room. At some point, it became living quarters for the pool manager. It was a way to get a good person to take the job. They lived there during the summer months up until the late '60s.

Top: Roosevelt Fieldhouse, built in 1932 as a WPA project. *From* Glenview, the First Centennial.

Bottom: Dancing classes inside Roosevelt Fieldhouse. *From* Glenview, the First Centennial.

133

The Park District office was located upstairs on the east side of the building, where it housed the necessary locker rooms and support facilities for the pool, including a manager's office, concession stand, filter room and storage. The downstairs area of the building included storage, the large filter room, a walk-in safe and locker rooms for the pool and baseball players in the park, who would enter and exit via the stairs located on the northeast side of the building. As time went on, the building underwent a number of renovations, including an addition in each pool locker room of a basket room. Pool-goers would come to the pool, change into their suits and put their street clothes into a wire basket. They received a metal pin with a stamped basket number and pinned it to their suit. When they finished swimming, they would return the pin for the appropriate basket. In about 1983, the district removed the baskets and racks and put in lockers.

THE BEACH AWAY FROM THE LAKE

It is believed the design for Roosevelt Park Pool was created by a Mr. Hunter, an architect who sold the plans to the WPA. They might have been commissioned by the WPA, which used the plans to build more than a dozen pools throughout the Midwest. Construction of the pool began in 1938. It was revolutionary in that it was the first round zero-depth public pool ever designed. Instead of a concrete deck to surround Glenview's new pool, sand overlaid the deck to give it a beach-like feeling.

An in-water metal fence surrounded the deep end, with gate-like openings allowing entrance to the deep end. It was an unspoken rule that before a child could swim in the deep end, one of the guards would need to watch the little one swim from the fence to the island and then back to the fence. Because it was so nerve-wracking for a kid, usually the most affable guard was chosen for the test. It was a real problem when the kid's favorite guard was overseeing the diving area.

THE DEEP END

In the middle of the pool was the island, a round roofed structure supporting a lifeguard stand and four diving boards, including a high dive and a springboard. Lines for the diving boards could be congested, and only one person was allowed on at a time. The boys were also doing

Building the island at Roosevelt Pool. *From "Roots: A Glenview Story."*

cannonballs while the poor little girls waited in line, pulling on their tight little bathing caps. One side of the island was free and open from boards, nudging new little divers practicing avoiding belly flops. With all the wet kids climbing on and off, plenty of slipping was going on. And that wasn't all that was slipping.

There was a small access door to the bottom with windows to view into the deep water. It was designed as a guard station to watch if anyone was in distress. It was one of those good ideas that made sense at the time, but it was small, dank, cold and claustrophobic down there. The other issue was that when diving, suits might slip a bit, so that was the end of that experiment.

Besides the lifeguard seat on the island, four guard stands with adjustable umbrellas protected the deep end. Other guards walked around the perimeter watching the kids like hawks or, in the case of the female guards, like mother hens. Usually, they were teenagers, lording their positions. They could really yell, shouting "YOU!" If a kid, usually a boy, was too obnoxious, the "YOU" would be accompanied by a pointed finger and a stern look toward the locker rooms. One time, a twelve-year-old took a lick from her sister's popsicle while the sister sat on the concession deck, which was not located in the pool area. (The architects and parents took the one-hour rule of resting after eating thoroughly seriously.) The popsicle-licking swimmer got the "YOU!" with the pointy finger and stern look. Out she went.

The island at Roosevelt Pool on a typical summer day. *From Glenview, the First Centennial.*

When the pool was constructed, concrete sections were poured to keep the pool from cracking, creating something akin to a checkerboard with the corners cut off. While this design prevented severe cracking, the pool tank sections did move some, especially during the freeze and thaw cycles of winter and spring. When originally built, the joints were sealed with tar. The problem was that when things warmed up and expansion took place, the concrete pool sections would shift and push tar up into the pool tank. Kids would come out of the pool with tar on their suits and little bodies. The only way to remove the tar was with gasoline—not a very safe practice! When waterproof caulk became available, some of the tar was taken out, and caulk was put in every joint. In the mid-'80s, the pool, which had likely been painted dozens of times over the years, was sandblasted down to the concrete, and all the tar was removed.

To treat and filter the pool, there were twenty-four inlets for water to return to the shallow areas of the pool. At the edge of the pool where the water met the sand, these inlets were capped with a concrete base topped by an Art Deco–style planter stand and planter. Each of the planters was filled with flowers each summer. Inside the cast-iron planter stands were three floodlights with red, white and blue bulbs, activated by a control box inside the tunnel entrance. A rotating wheel with three contacts affixed to it would slowly turn. Contact would be made with the first paddle, and all the white lights would come on. As the wheel moved, the next paddle would make contact, and the red lights would come on, then the blue, the red and the white again.

When the pool was first built, a fence surrounded the pool edge, allowing entry to the pool in four or five places. This was done to limit the amount of sand getting into the pool, as it caused all sorts of issues, the biggest one being that the sand migrated to the pool bottom drains. It traveled through three large vents filled with varying grades of gravel and sand, which trapped dirt and leaves. The additional sand from the decks eventually clogged the filters, and they had to be opened and dug out. This and the onset of polio convinced the district to switch the deck to concrete.

Four slides, two straight and two bumpy, equidistant in the shallow areas, were modified from metal playground slides to fit the slope of the pool. A line was plumbed to the top of the slide, providing trickling water to make the slides faster and cool them down from the sun.

The filter room that strained the water from the pool and injected chemicals into the water was in the basement directly under the main room and included several storage areas. A tunnel went from the filter room directly south, under the deck, and all the way to the deep end, where it ended. Roughly twelve inches of concrete was all that separated the tunnel from the deep middle section of the pool. The purpose of the tunnel was to provide easy access to the filter room, allowing workers to monitor the condition of piping and repair it as needed. Without the tunnel, the deck would have had to be dug up to get to any leaks.

ICE SKATING ON THE POOL

In the winter, the facility was used for ice skating. The pool water was not emptied to prevent deep frost from raising it out of the ground. Skaters used the locker rooms to put on their skates and would go out to skate around the pool. The problem was that the pool leaked pretty much from day one. Even in the off-season, staff would have to go into the filter room and turn on the fill valve to raise the water level. The water was pumped in from the deep area recirculation pipes. Long story short, the water was turned on one day when there was a gap between the ice and water line. The force of the water coming into the pool from the bottom hit the bottom of the ice cover and melted some of it. That day, the maintenance man drove on the frozen surface to brush off the ice shavings made from skate blades. The vehicle drove over a thin area in the ice and broke through, going to the bottom of the pool. That was the end of skating in the pool in the winter! Luckily, he was unhurt.

Glenview was growing and, in the late '50s, generated crowds so big that the pool would hit its 1,500-bather capacity every day. The solution was to change the two four-hour sessions into three two-hour sessions. There were still long lines stretching all the way to Fir Street. The feisty swimmers learned to time their early exit from the first session and hightail to the line in time to get in on the second afternoon session. This condition was the genesis of building a second pool at the new Flick Park on the fast-growing west side of town. Flick Pool opened in 1963.

Hopping the fence late at night to go swimming was a rite of passage for many a Glenview teen. For the most part it was harmless, but there were occasional pool hoppers who would vandalize the pool, which was very unfortunate. This was probably one of the reasons the pool manager was offered housing in the building. Every summer, as part of the pool-hopping tradition, some gross person would leave their mark on the guard chair on the top of the island. They were referred to as the "Mad Pooper." Enough said.

The Annual Water Show

The highlight at Roosevelt Pool was the Annual Water Show. The staff would write a script around a chosen theme such as superheroes, circus or cops and robbers. The parks crew took the bleachers from softball fields and put them on the pool decks. Each pool had a sizeable drive-through gate for maintenance and emergency vehicles, making it easy to place the bleachers. Large spotlights were rented and put on the locker room roofs. The shows were about a half-hour long and included skits, diving exhibitions and a synchronized swimming display by the town's teenagers. There were diving board tricks and pranks worked in a diving exhibition. The divers and a few "clown divers" would execute well-choreographed dives that ended up in belly flops and other disaster landings.

The two most popular events were lifeguard jousting and the famous fire dive. The guard jousting involved two guards from each pool staff competing for bragging rights. They would start at opposite ends of the pool and paddle a canoe to the middle, where they met. At that point, the guard on the front of each canoe would take out their jousting pole, which was really a long aluminum pool vacuum pole with a foam ball at the end. They would joust until one or the other was knocked into the water. The best two out of three was declared the winner.

Every show closed with the Fire Dive. This involved a dramatic climb by the lifeguard to the top ring of the island roof, hamming it up and making it look scarier than it was. Another guard would throw a mixture of gasoline and kerosene into the pool below the diver and light the pool on fire. The gasp from the audience was always fun. After some trepidation and buildup of drama for effect, the guard would execute a perfect swan dive through the ten-foot-high flames. There were years when the staff would get creative and put a scuba tank at the bottom of the pool so the guard could stay below the surface after the dive. The crowd would go wild, and the kids would start to get nervous. The manager would be on the public address system directing other guards to get the backboard and go in to rescue the diver, at which point, he or she would pop through the surface to thunderous applause.

In reality, the diver didn't leap straight into the fire. Instead, he would dive to the left from the island, toward the baseball field. That gave the audience a great look at the fire and the diver. The key was for the person throwing the gas/kerosene mixture to toss it in the pool in an arc. This would give the impression that the whole pool was on fire, although the area directly under the diver was clear.

GOLDFISH DAY

An end-of-year tradition started in the mid-'50s when a couple thousand goldfish were put into the pool at the 3:00 p.m. safety break. Capacity crowds circled the pool waiting for the manager to give the go sign. It seemed like a million kids rushed into the pool with their plastic fish-catching bags, searching for a new pet for their goldfish bowls. It rarely took more than thirty minutes for the fish to be caught, and the staff always held extra fish

Goldfish Day at Roosevelt Park Pool. Notice the slide in the top photo. *From* Glenview, the First Centennial.

in reserve for little kids who didn't catch one. Some fish would last for a week, and others were reported to have lived for years. There would always be a few fish that would hide in the deep drains and often would be found swimming in the pool the next spring. Swimming with the fish went until the state department of public health deemed it inappropriate in the late '90s.

THE POOL'S EVENTUAL DEMISE

By the '80s, the pool facility was really beginning to show its age. Pools in the Midwest are expected to last thirty-five to forty years. Roosevelt Pool had been in constant operation for forty-five years. The building was also in need of major upgrades and repairs. Over the course of several years, the locker rooms were renovated, and the pool was repaired to the degree possible. Unfortunately, regulations and standards for public pools had evolved over time to make the Roosevelt facility significantly out of code. If major work was not done to the pool, the grandfather clause in the pool code allowed the pool to continue to operate. By the late '80s and early '90s, the four playground slides had finally degraded to the point where they needed to be removed. The pool code didn't allow for new slides to go in due to the water depth and proximity to the deep-water fence. The tall pole that held the island roof structure and lights began to rust through and had to be removed. The original filters were cut up and removed in lieu of more efficient modern filter equipment, and a slew of other cosmetic repairs was made. But by 2003, it was clear that the pool was near the end of its useful life. The pool tank leaked so badly that nearly three million gallons of water were lost in a single season—roughly six times the pool's capacity. In 2004, a referendum was held to renovate or replace Roosevelt Pool and Flick Pool, which had reached its forty-first season of service. The referendum passed, and the pools were closed in late August 2004. Through a coordinated effort, the park district removed and replaced the facilities in nine months, opening in mid-June 2005. Updated play pieces were installed, including a preschool slide and some water-spraying elephants, named Eleanor, Teddy and Franklin in a naming contest. Studies found that Roosevelt Pool had over 3 million visitors and swimming lessons for at least 53,500 children in its sixty-four years of service.

Roosevelt Pool had come a long way. So has Glenview.

NOTES

Chapter 1

1. Ernst, "Roots: A Glenview Story," 51; Head, *Glenview at 75*.
2. "Early Settler in Northfield," *Daily Herald*, May 22, 1925, 14; Yoder, *Taverns and Travelers*, 132; Gale, Digital Research Library of Illinois History; DeLuca, "Stagecoach Sustained Commerce and Communications"; Ernst, "Roots: A Glenview Story," 11.
3. Head, *Glenview at 75*, 40–41; Ernst, "Roots: A Glenview Story," 30, 31; Rugen, *Growing Up with Glenview*.
4. Trapp, *Destiny of Undying Greatness*; "World War 1 Casualties"; Klein, "False Armistice"; *Chicago Tribune*, "Truce Is Not Yet Signed," November 8, 1918, 1, 3; Smith, "Reuters and the False Armistice"; *Chicago Tribune*, "Great War Ends," November 11, 1918, 1; *Chicago Tribune*, "Chicago Makes Kaiser's Woke Wild Bedlam; Million People Surge Loop in Biggest Celebration," November 12, 1918, 3; *Chicago Tribune*, "'Thish Ish on Me' Say Women, Feet on Bar Rail," November 12, 1918, 9.
5. Glazets, *Glenview, the First Centennial*, 42; *Daily Herald*, November 29, 1918, 5; "Officials Find Hupmobiles Need No Brake Testing," *Niles Center Press*, n.d.; "Local Hupmobile Agent Urges Inspection of Brakes," *San Pedro News Pilot*, n.d.
6. Anderson, "Crack Open an Old One"; Musson, *D.G. Yuengling & Son*.

Chapter 2

7. Gale, Digital Research Library of Illinois History; Hoynes et al., "New Trier Township," 5, 6.

8. Okrent, *Last Call*, 32; Burns, *Prohibition*; Kerr, *Organized for Prohibition*, 115–22; Thompson, "Meet the Doctor"; Sutcliffe, "Benjamin Franklin"; Klein, "Brief History of Presidential Drinking"; Abrams, *Party Like a President*, 4, 7, 17; Okrent, *Last Call*, 31; White, "Alcohol as Medicine and Poison."

9. Ohio History Central, "Temperance Movement"; Okrent, *Last Call*, 75; Stack, "Concise History of America's Brewing Industry"; Maine, an Encyclopedia, "Alcohol"; Eschner, "Why Was Maine the First State to Try Prohibition?"

10. Hibbard, *Roots, a Glenview Story*, 6; Okrent, *Last Call*, 51.

11. Schmidt, "On the Road to Women's Suffrage"; Wikipedia, "Frances Willard."

12. Behr, *Prohibition*, 271, 279–83; McKenna, "Carry Nation"; Blakemoore, "Prohibitionist Carry Nation Smashes Bar."

13. Arthur Sears Henning, "Dry League Is Mighty Engine of Propaganda," *Chicago Tribune*, July 11, 1927, 1; Wikipedia, "Wayne Wheeler"; Wikipedia, "Anti-Saloon League"; Okrent, "Wayne B. Wheeler"; Westerville Public Library, "Why Westerville?"; Gambrinus, editorial, "What Are the Limits of Prohibition?" *Chicago Tribune*, September 26, 1921, 8; McGirr, *War on Alcohol*, 233.

14. Hoynes et al., "New Trier Township,"6; McGirr, *War on Alcohol*, 42, 50.

15. Wilmette Historical Museum; "Four-Mile Limit Law Held Valid," *NorthShore News*, August 6, 1904; "Gross Point Bars Closed for First Time in History," *Chicago Tribune*, May 8, 1909, 6; "Citizens Association vs. Blind Pigs," *Local News*, April 21, 1916, 1; Fulton, "I'll Drink to That"; "They Doused the Glim," *Illinois Issue*, May 14, 1909; "Steffins Fined Two Hundred and Costs," *Lake Shore News*, November 20, 1914, 1; "Saloon War Proves Fatal; Gross Point Man a Suicide Following a Crusade Against His Place," *Chicago Tribune*, January 3, 1911, 9.

16. "Liquor's Knell to Toll in U.S. at Midnight: Last Rites Joyless, Though Law Nods," *Chicago Tribune*, January 16, 1920, 1; *Daily Herald*, January 30, 1920, 1.

17. "Mayor McCullen Appoints New Motorcycle 'Cop,'" *Daily Herald*, May 9, 1924, 13; "Bride Weeps Beery Tears over License," *Daily Herald*, June 13, 1924, 9.

Chapter 3

18. "Violence Stains Rural Bohemia's 10 Year History," *Chicago Tribune*, March 26, 1935, 3.

19. Luc, *Northbrook*, 48; Judy Hughes, personal communication, September 15, 2020.

20. Russell, "Road House."

21. Binder, *Al Capone's Beer Wars*, 74.

22. Head, "History of Law and Order in Glenview."

23. Hibbard, *Roots, a Glenview Story*, 49.

24. E.F. Connor, letter to the editor, *Chicago Tribune*, January 22, 1920, 6.

25. "Boys Grape Juice Jag Makes Trouble for Dealer," *Chicago Tribune*, September 21, 1921, 1.

26. "Liquor's Knell to Toll in U.S. at Midnight," *Chicago Tribune*, January 16, 1920, 1.

27. Franklin, *What Prohibition Has Done to America*.

28. "Resigns," *Chicago Tribune*, October 29, 1920, 1.

29. Glenview State Bank History, gsb.com. Shortly after its centennial in 2021, the Glenview State Bank merged with Busey Bank, and GSB banking centers became branches of Busey Bank Corporation. "First Busey Corporation," GlobeNewswire; Glazets, *Glenview, the First Centennial*, 66; "Cashier's Mysterious Murder," *Chicago Tribune*, September 25, 1921, 3; "Glen View Bank Cashier Is Shot Dead by Bandits," *Chicago Tribune*, September 25, 1921, 3; "How Bank Cashier Was Murdered," *Daily Herald*, September 30, 1921, 3; "Finger Prints in Glen View," *Chicago Tribune*, September 29, 1921, 1; "Card of Thanks," *Daily Herald*, October 28, 1921, 9.

30. Roos, "How Prohibition Put the 'Organized' in Organized Crime."

31. Wikipedia, "Johnny Torrio."

32. Russell, "Road House"; "Bootlegger's Story," *New Yorker*; Batchelor, "Bootlegging"; Andrews, "10 Things You Should Know About Prohibition."

33. Wikipedia, "Rum-running"; Mejia, "Lucrative Business of Prescribing Booze"; ad, "How a National Reputation Grew Out of a Nickel Raise in Price," *Chicago Tribune*, June 18, 1929, 28; Hines, "How Jewish Bootleggers Saved the Day during Prohibition"; Teeter, "How Wine Bricks Saved the U.S. Wine Industry"; Mob Museum, "Bootleggers and Bathtub Gin"; Andrews, "10 Things You Should Know About Prohibition"; McGirr, *War on Alcohol*, 52.

34. "Ed Kelly Dies in Chicago; Well Known Hotel Man," *Waukegan Daily Sun*, November 5, 1920, 1; Mary Kelly and Jane Andersen Ruschli, personal communications; Dretske, "Aptikisic—Half Day"; "Man Run Over by Heavy Wagon," *Waukegan Daily Sun*, May 6, 1912, 1; "Arrest Two Men Charged with an Attempted Murder," *Waukegan Daily Sun*, August 29, 1912, 1, 5; "Seek Five Mile Limit Dry Zone about Training Station," *Waukegan Daily Sun*, June 5, 1914, 1, 3; "Village Council Passes Ordinance Whereby One Can't Even LOOK at Booze," *Waukegan Daily Sun*, June 3, 1914, 1; "Daniels Favors 'Dry Zone' for Naval Training School," *Chicago Tribune*, June 5, 1914, 15; "Saloonists Arraigned Here Today," *Waukegan Daily Sun*, June 5, 1914, 1; "Not Allowed to Sell Two Per Cent in the Dry Towns," *Waukegan Daily Sun*, June 5, 1914, 1; "Supervisors of Co. Powerless to Act on Evidence," *Waukegan Daily Sun*, June 16, 1917, 1.

35. "Orchestra Leader Praises Duffy's," *Waukegan Daily Sun*, April 6, 1917, 11; "For Home Use, Get Your Beer Direct," *Waukegan Daily Sun*, April 27, 1916, 1.

36. McElroy, "Story of How Moonshiners Created the Performance Car"; Klein, "How Prohibition Gave Birth to Nascar."

37. George R. Pinkowski Jr., personal communication, June 2021; Schneider, information on Matthew Hoffman; Touhy, *Stolen Years*, 45–52.

38. Pinkowski, "Biography of the Gross Point Bootlegger," 7–17; Schneider, Charlie Bohn interview, October 18, 1990; Schneider, interview with Max Reimer, August 16, 1990; Schneider, interview with Elmer Werhane, April 13, 15, 1991; Pinkowski, personal communication from Margaret Schoenbeck; Gouldsbury, email to the author; Ruschli, personal communication.

Chapter 4

39. Russell, "Road House."

40. Silsbee, "This Hotel Kept All the Secrets"; Faig, *Tearney Family*, 3; ad, *Daily Herald*, October 7, 1923, 73; Schreiber, Werhane interview; ad, *Chicago Tribune*, September 9, 1923, 14; "Garden of Allah Host to Players," *Cook County Herald*, May 22, 1925, 14; "Put Out Garden of Allah Blaze of Unknown Origin," *Daily Herald*, September 4, 1925, 12; ad, *Chicago Tribune*, June 18, 1929, 43; Schreiber, Werhane interview.

41. "Announcement," *Daily Herald*, November 2, 1923, 8; "Glenview Couple Wed at Morton Will Reside Here," *Daily Herald*, June 20, 1924, 1; "No Dull Moments at Bill Fischer's Over the Fourth," *Daily Herald*, July 4, 1924, 7; "Fischer's Eat Shop Is Popular Place with Motor Fans," *Daily Herald*, July 18, 1924, 24; "W.H. Fischer Lets Contract for Larger Dance Hall Addition," *Daily Herald*, February 27, 1925, 13; "New Reflectory [*sic*] and Ball Room to Open in the Near Future," *Daily Herald*, May 25, 1925, 14; "Great Plans Made for Opening of New Ball Room," *Daily Herald*, June 5, 1925, 5; "Glenview Bowlers in First Annual Banquet," *Daily Herald*, June 5, 1925, 5; ad, "The W.H. Fisher Ball Room," *Daily Herald*, June 5, 1925, 5; "The Four Seasons," *Daily Herald*, July 3, 1925, 4; "Four Seasons to Be Mad Popular for This Winter," *Daily Herald*, August 28, 1925, 9; ad, "The Four Seasons," *Daily Herald*, September 18, 1925, 17; "Members of Revue Cast Have a Repast at Fisher's," *Daily Herald*, September 18, 1925, 17; ad, "The Four Seasons," *Daily Herald*, July 23, 1926, 17; "Four Seasons," *Daily Herald*, July 22, 1928, 63; "Violence Stains Rural Bohemia's 10 Year History," *Chicago Tribune*, March 26, 1935, 3.

42. "Villa Venice Attracts the Elite," *Chicago Tribune*, July 22, 1928, 63; Craig, "Villa Venice."

43. Russell, "Road House."

44. Richard Larson, personal communication; McIntyre and McIntyre, "Wheeling through the Years"; Dawson, *Glenview*, 50; Markey, "If I May So"; "Moulin Rouge to Be Loop's Luxurious Café," *Chicago Tribune*, October 30, 1921, 22; ad, *Chicago Tribune*, May 29, 1923, 19; ad, *Chicago Tribune*, July 3, 1923, 15; "Cackling Saved Rome but Not These Revelers," *Chicago Tribune*, July 9, 1923, 3; ad, *Chicago Tribune*, June 12, 1924, 23; ad, *Chicago Tribune*, July 25, 1925, 11; ad, *Chicago Tribune*, May 26, 1928, 17; "Villa Venice Attracts the Elite," *Chicago*

Tribune, July 22, 1928, 63; Herb Lyon, "Tower Ticker Column," *Chicago Tribune*, October 12, 1956, 37.

45. Grossman, "In 1962, Chicago Mob Boss Had Sinatra Singing His Way," 25; "Blaze Sweeps Villa Venice," *Chicago Tribune*, March 5, 1967, 1.

46. "Grove Pavilion Grand Dance," *Daily Herald*, June 1, 1923, 1; Schreiber, interview with Ed Schuett and Elmer Werhane, April 13–15, 1991.

47. "It Is Now the Glenview Inn," *Daily Herald* (Arlington Heights), April 11, 1924, 12; ad, *Daily Herald*, February 8, 1924; "Announcement," *Daily Herald*, April 25, 1924, 7; "Additional Glenview," *Daily Herald*, May 9, 1924, 16; "Additional Glenview," *Daily Herald* (Arlington Heights), April 11, 1924, 2; "In the Shops of Glenview," *Daily Herald*, April 25, 1924; ad, *Daily Herald*, July 3, 1925, 4.

48. Hyssey-Arntson and Leary, *Wilmette*, 17; "1933 Meier's Tavern," *North Shore Magazine*; Tommy Reece, personal communication; Gus Pappas, personal communication; *Daily Herald* (Arlington Heights), February 6, 1925, 12; Sally Masterson Landri, personal communication; Kogan, "For 70 Years, Meier's Tavern."

49. "26 Folk Nabbed in Dry Roads on 8 Roadhouses," *Chicago Tribune*, June 8, 1924, 3; "30 Roadhouses Ask Licenses," *Palatine Enterprise*, October 30, 1925, 17.

50. "Membership in a Political Club Does Not Save Bootlegger," *Palatine Enterprise*, November 13, 1925, 9.

51. Russell, "Road House"; Ruschli, personal communication; Landri, personal communication; Engels, "Frank Engels"; Jacoby, "Hackney's Story"; Karen Kelly Bohlke, personal communication, 1965–67.

52. Thrillist, "Hackney's"; Jacoby, "Hackney's Story"; Glazets, *Glenview, the First Centennial*, 44; Zeldes, "Hackney's"; Macushla, "Our Story."

53. Karen Kelly Bohlke, personal communication; *Daily Herald* (Arlington Heights), February 8, 1924, 1; "Dry Raiders Seize Liquor," *Chicago Tribune*, July 10, 1927; Ruschli, personal communication.

54. Glazets, *Glenview, the First Centennial*, 68; Faig, *Tearney Family*, 3; "Hit-Run Auto Kills Boy; Three Seized in Chase," *Chicago Tribune*, August 23, 1936, 8.

Chapter 5

55. *Niles Center Press*, May 18, 1928, 1.

56. *Niles Center Press*, November 9, 1928, 1.

57. Touhy, *Stolen Years*, 45–52.

58. Famous People, "Bugs Moran Biography"; Keefe, *Man Who Got Away*, 26; Chicago Master Cleaners and Dyers Association, "To the Public," *Chicago Tribune*, July 2, 1928, 18.

59. Allsop, *Bootlegger in Their Era*, 138–39; Helmer and Bilek, *St. Valentine's Day Massacre*, 140; Binder, *Al Capone's Beer Wars*, 198–99; Coates, *St. Valentine's Day Massacre*.

60. Faig, *Tearney Family*, 5–6; "Garden of Allah Manager Shot by Gang of Bandits," *Chicago Tribune*, September 4, 1929, 1; "Hospital Visit Called Attempt to Kill Tearney," *Chicago Tribune*, September 5, 1929, 2; Coppola, *The Godfather*; Silsbee, "This Hotel Kept All the Secrets."

61. "Bomb Damages Resort; Blame Beer Gang War," *Chicago Tribune*, November 1, 1929, 1; "Café Near Air Race Field Raided by Drys; One Held," *Chicago Tribune*, August 28, 1930, 2.

62. "Hunt Bandits Who Killed 3 Women in Café," *Chicago Tribune*, November 24, 1930, 7; "Tavern Raiders Kill Broker Husband Slain on His Way to Stricken Wife," *Chicago Tribune*, November 26, 1930, 1; "City and County Police Hunt for Broker's Killers: Roadhouse Owner Tells of Raid by Bandits," *Chicago Tribune*, November 27, 1930, 10; "Rich Chicago Broker Slain by 5 Bandits: Broker Slain When He Is Slow Obeying Leader's Command," *Clinton Daily Journal and Public* (Clinton, IL), November 27, 1930, 1; "Son of Chicago Multimillionaire Laughs at Bandits: Broker Thinks Holdup Is a Joke and Is Killed," *Republican-Northwestern* (Belvidere, IL), November 28, 1930, 1; "Capture Eight in Roundup of Robbery Gang," *Chicago Tribune*, February 15, 1931, 1, 2; "Big Robberies Held Solved in Grilling of Captive Trio," *Chicago Tribune*, February 17, 1931, 4; "Suspect Is Shot; 6 Men, 3 Women Seized in Flat," *Chicago Tribune*, November 5, 1931, 7; "Broker Slaying Is Re-enacted by Young Bandit—Winnetka Mother Claims Son Is Innocent," *Chicago Tribune*, November 7, 1931, 3; "Youth of 17 Held on Murder Charge," *Journal Gazette* (Mattoon, IL), November 7, 1931, 1; "Boy Confesses to Police How He Killed Man," *The Times* (Streator, IL), November 7, 1931, 1; "Young Slayer Arraigned in Killing of Banker," *Chicago Tribune*, November 11, 1931, 19; "Dismiss Murder Charge Against Winnetka Youth," *Chicago Tribune*, April 15, 1932, 10.

63. Schneider, Charlie Bohn interview; Schneider, information on Matthew Hoffman/Roger Touhy; Schneider, Elmer Werhane interview; Herion, *Touhy vs. Capone*, 42; Schneider, Ed Schuett interview; Burrough, *Public Enemies*, 143; "Beer Peddler Is Slain in Trap Near Roadhouse: Body Carried Off and Left in Field: Two Youths Find Bullet Ridden Body," *Chicago Tribune*, August 1, 1931, 3, 12; "Beer Peddler Found Murdered—Two Youths Find Bullet Ridden Body—Wilmette Beer Agent Missing Since Thursday Night Found Murdered in Corn Field Near Half Day Last Night," *Waukegan News-Sun*, August 1, 1931, 1, 2; "Auto of Murdered Beer Agent Found," *Waukegan News-Sun*, August 3, 1931, 12; "Beer Quarrel Is Believed Cause of Death," *Daily Chronicle* (DeKalb, IL), August 1, 1931, 2; "Matt Hoffman Beer Maker Is Taken for a Ride," *The Times* (Streator, IL), August 1, 1931, 1; "War of Rivals in Beer War Is Blamed for Death," *Daily Republican-Register* (Mount Carmel, IL), August 1, 1931, 4; *Greater Niles Center News*, August 7, 1931, 1, 2; Mary Welch, personal communication, October 2021; "Wilmette Man Is Show Down in Mystery Attack," *Chicago*

Tribune, August 11, 1931, 2; "Wilmette Ride Victim Found to Have Record—Reveal His Past with Fingerprints," *Chicago Tribune*, August 12, 1931, 3; "Widow Denies Police Version of Dumont Ride," *Chicago Tribune*, August 13, 1931, 7; "Link Hoffman Dumont Deaths—Chicago Detectives Believe Chicago and Local Murders Have Connection," *Waukegan News-Sun*, August 12, 1931, 1; Binder, *Al Capone's Beer Wars*, 232–35; Schneider, Charlie Bohn interview; Herion, *Touhy vs. Capone*, 121.

64. Glazets, *Glenview, the First Centennial*, 66; "Found Guilty in Slaying of Federal Agent," *Chicago Tribune*, March 26, 1935, 1; Nickel and Helmer, *Baby Face Nelson*, 371; Burrough, *Public Enemies*, 143; FBI, "Byte Out of History."

65. "Tavern Again Coming Back Into Its Own," *Chicago Tribune*, May 1, 1928, 8; "Dry Era Knocks Joy from Dining, Rector Asserts," *Chicago Tribune*, May 25, 1928, 14; "U.S. Prohibition Farce to British Woman Official," *Chicago Tribune*, October 21, 1929, 6; "Sheriff Explains: If Citizens Would Take More Interest, Conditions Would Be Better," *Chicago Tribune*, October 29, 1929, 1; "Enjoying a Nip No Crime, Says Senator Blease," *Chicago Tribune*, October 21, 1929, 12.

Chapter 6

66. "Hard Times in Illinois."

67. Beverly Roberts Dawson, personal communication, 2021; Liz Hebson, personal communication, 2020–21; Landri, personal communication, 2021.

68. Wikipedia, "1932 United States Presidential Election"; "1932 United States Presidential Election," *Chicago Tribune*, November 9, 1932, 1; McGirr, *War on Alcohol*, 15–19, 246; Klein, "FDR Legalizes Sale of Beer and Wine"; Okrent, *Last Call*, 374; "State Starts Drive on Taverns without Liquor Licenses," *Daily Herald*, July 20, 1934, 1.

69. *Glenview View*, July 20, 1934, 1.

70. Jessica Cantarelli, "Locals Remember Wayside Inn as Glenview Landmark," October 26, 2009, triblocal.com/glenview.com; Larry Townsend, "Matty's Supper Club Legacy Ably Upheld," *Chicago Tribune*, January 17, 1997; Dawson, *Glenview*, 72; Glazets, *Glenview, the First Centennial*, 43.

71. Alcatraz History, "Al Capone at Alcatraz."

72. Wikipedia, "Bugs Moran."

73. Wikipedia, "Roger Touhy."

74. Binder, *Al Capone's Beer Wars*, 267.

75. James O'Donnell Bennett, "Youths Taming Waste Areas of Skokie Marsh: 822 Workers Thrive Under Army's Care," *Chicago Tribune*, September 4, 1933, 10, 28; Hoynes et al., "New Trier Township," 2; "2,000 CCC Men Reclaiming 900 Swampy Acres: Making a Great Park in Skokie Valley," *Chicago Sunday Tribune*, February 18, 1934, 3.

76. Awalt, "Recollections of the Banking Crisis"; "Glenview State Bank Reopened March 29," *Arlington Heights Herald*, March 31, 1933, 1.

77. *Glenview View*, January 1, 1937.

78. Bob Quill, personal communications, August 19, 2020–October 1, 2020.

BIBLIOGRAPHY

Books

Abadinsky, Howard. *Organized Crime.* Chicago: Thompson-Wadsworth, 2003.

Abrams, Brian. *Party Like a President: True Tales of Inebriations, Lechery, and Mischief from the Oval Office.* New York: Workman Publishing, 2015.

Achorn, Edward. *The Summer of Beer and Whiskey: How Brewers, Barkeeps, Rowdies, Immigrants and a Wild Pennant Fight Made Baseball America's Game.* New York: Public Affairs, 2013.

Allen, Frederick Lewis. *Only Yesterday: An Informal History of the 1920s.* New York: Open Road Integrated Media, 2015.

Allsop, Kenneth. *The Bootlegger in Their Era.* Garden City, NY: Doubleday, 1961.

Behr, Edward. *Prohibition: Thirteen Years That Changed America.* New York: Arcade Publishing, 1996.

Binder, John L. *Al Capone's Beer Wars: A Complete History of Organized Crime in Chicago During Prohibition.* Amherst, NY: Prometheus Books, 2017.

Blumenthal, Karen. *Bootleg Murder, Moonshine, and the Lawless Years of Prohibition.* New York: Roaring Brook Press, 2011.

Burrough, Bryan. *Public Enemies: America's Greatest Crime Wave and the Birth of the FBI, 1933–34.* New York: Penguin Books, 2004.

Coates, Tim, ed. *The St. Valentine's Day Massacre, 1929.* London: Stationery Office, 2001.

Dawson, Beverly Roberts. *Glenview.* Charleston, SC: Arcadia Publishing, 2008.

———. *Glenview Naval Air Station.* Charleston, SC: Arcadia Publishing, 2007.

Faig, Ken, Jr. *The Tearney Family and Glenview's Garden of Allah.* Glenview, IL: Swainwood Books, 2018.

Franklin, Fabian. *What Prohibition Has Done to America.* 1922. Repr., Monee, IL: 2021.

Gately, Iain. *Drink: A Cultural History of Alcohol.* New York: Gotham Books, 2008.

Glazets, Nancy LaMair, ed. *Glenview, the First Centennial.* Glenview, IL: Glenview Centennial Commission, Paul H. Thomas, Publisher, 1999.

Grossman, James R., Ann Durkin Keating and Janice L. Reiff, eds. *The Encyclopedia of Chicago.* Chicago: University of Chicago Press, 2004.

Harris, Neil. *The Chicagoan: A Lost Magazine of the Jazz Age.* Chicago: University of Chicago Press, 2008.

Head, Mrs. Marshall, ed. *Glenview at 75, 1899–1874: Diamond Anniversary, July 4-5-6, 1974.* N.p.: Union Press, Inc., 1974.

Helmer, William J., and Arthur J. Bilek. *The St. Valentine's Day Massacre.* Nashville, TN: Cumberland House, 2004.

Herion, Donald H. *Touhy vs. Capone.* Charleston, SC: The History Press, 2017.

Hibbard, Richard L., et al. *Roots, a Glenview Story.* N.p.: published by the Souvenir Book Committee, 1976.

Hyssey-Arntson, Kathy, and Patrick Leary. *Wilmette.* Charleston, SC: Arcadia Publishing, 2012.

Johns, Richard E. *Past, Present, Future: Planning Report: Marking the Fiftieth Anniversary of the Glenview Park District, Cook County, IL, 1927–1977.* Glenview, IL: Glenview Park District, 1977.

Keefe, Rose. *The Man Who Got Away: The Bugs Moran Story, a Biography.* Nashville, TN: Cumberland House, 2005, iBook.

Kerr, K. Austin. *Organized for Prohibition: A New History of the Anti-Saloon League.* New Haven, CT: Yale University Press, 1985.

Kyvig, David E. *Repealing National Prohibition.* Kent, OH: Kent State University Press, 2000.

Lewis, Michael, and Richard F. Hamm, eds. *The Distilled Truth About American's Anti-Alcohol Crusade.* Baton Rouge: Louisiana State University Press, 2020.

Luc, Katie Angell, and Judith Jaclyn Hughes. *Northbrook.* Charleston, SC: Arcadia Publishing, 2008.

Lyle, John H. *The Dry and Lawless Years.* Englewood Cliffs, NJ: Prentice-Hall, 1960.

McClellan, Michelle L. *Lady Lushes: Gender, Alcoholism, and Medicine in Modern America.* New Brunswick, NJ: Rutgers University Press, 2017.

McGirr, Lisa. *The War on Alcohol: Prohibition and the Rise of the American State.* New York: W.W. Norton, 2016.

Murdock, Catherine Gilbert. *Domesticating Drink: Women, Men, and Alcohol in America, 1870–1940 (Gender Relations in the American Experience).* Baltimore, MD: Johns Hopkins University Press, 1998.

Musson, Robert, A., MD. *D.G. Yuengling & Son, Inc.* Charleston, SC: Arcadia Publishing, 2013.

Nickel, Steven, and William J. Helmer. *Baby Face Nelson: Portrait of a Public Enemy.* Nashville, TN: Cumberland House, 2002.

Okrent, Daniel. *Last Call: The Rise and Fall of Prohibition.* New York: Scribner, 2011.

Pinkowski, George R. "Biography of the Gross Point Bootlegger." Unpublished manuscript, 2017.

Rorabaugh, W.J. *The Alcoholic Republic: An American Tradition.* New York: Oxford University Press, 1929.

Rugen, Fred A. *Growing Up with Glenview.* N.p.: Betty Rugen Shutter, under Berne Copyright Convention, 2010.

Salinger, Sharon V. *Taverns and Drinking in Early America.* Baltimore, MD: Johns Hopkins University Press, 2002.

Sismondo, Christine. *America Walks into a Bar: A Spirited History of Taverns and Saloons, Speakeasies and Grog Shops.* New York: Oxford University Press, 2011.

Touhy, Roger. *The Stolen Years.* New York: Litchfield Literary Books, 1959.

Trapp, Mark M. *A Destiny of Undying Greatness: Kiffen Rockwell and the Boys Who Remembered Lafayette.* Chicago: System D. Publishing Company, 2019.

Yoder, Paton. *Taverns and Travelers: Inns of the Early Midwest.* Bloomington: Indiana University Press, 1969.

Archives, Journals, Magazines, Websites and Other Sources

Adams, Samuel Hopkins. "My Bootlegger." *Collier's*, September 17, 1921. Reprinted in *A Calvacade of Collier's*, edited by Kenneth McArdle. New York: A.S. Barnes, Inc., 1959.

Alcatraz History. "Al Capone at Alcatraz." www.alcatrazhistory.com/cap1.htm.

Alexander, Dave. Legends of America. legendsofamerica.com.

Anderson, L.V. "Crack Open an Old One." *Slate*, October 22, 2014. slate.com/business/2014/10/worlds-oldest-breweries-an-unscientific-ranking-of-germanys-oldest-beers.html.

Andrews, Evan. "10 Things You Should Know About Prohibition." History, February 22, 2019. www.history.com/news/10-things-you-should-know-about-prohibition.

Awalt, Francis Gloyd. "Recollections of the Banking Crisis 1933." Autumn 1969. frasier.stlouis.org/title/recollections-banking-crisis-1933-3593.

Batchelor, Bob. "Bootlegging." Encyclopedia. www.encyclopedia.com/social-sciences-and-law/law/crime-and-law-enforcement/bootlegging.

Blakemoore, Erin. "Prohibitionist Carry Nation Smashes Bar." A&E Networks, December 10, 2018. history.com/news/carrieNation-temperance-prohibition-alcohol.

Byerly, Carol R. "War Losses (USA)." International Encyclopedia of the First World War, October 8, 2014. encyclopedia.1914-1918-online.net/article/war_losses_usa.

Church, Ralph E. "Something to Think About, American Ideals." *Northbrook News*, November 6, 1936.

Craig, J.W. "The Villa Venice: Albert 'Papa' Bouche: Revisited." Under Every Tombstone, December 1, 2020. undereverytombstone.blogspot.com/2020/12/the-villa-venice-albert-papa-bouche.html.

DeLuca, Richard. "Stagecoach Sustained Commerce and Communications in 1800s." Connecticut History, May 3, 2021. connecticuthistory.org/stagecoach-travel-sustained-commerce-and-communication-in-1800s.

Dretske, Diana, curator, Bess Bower Dunn Museum. "Aptikisic—Half Day." Email, March 25, 2011.

Engels, Frank. "Frank Engels: Growing Up in Glenview on Hackney's on Lake Property Since 1930." Information on Hackney's and Masterson family, n.d.

Ernst, Isabel, ed. "Roots: A Glenview Story." Glenview Bicentennial Commission, 1976.

Eschner, Kat. "Why Was Maine the First State to Try Prohibition?" *Smithsonian Magazine*, June 2, 2017. www.smithsonianmag.com/smart-news/maine-first-state-try-prohibition-180963503.

Famous People. "Bugs Moran Biography." www.thefamouspeople.com/profiles/bugs-moran-9478.php.

FBI. "A Byte Out of History: Man on the Run: The Last Hours of Baby Face Nelson." November 29, 2004. archives.fbi.gov/archives/news/stories/2004/november/nelson_112904.

Fulton, Jacob. "I'll Drink to That: A History of Alcohol and Temperance in Evanston." *Daily Northwestern*, May 14, 2020. dailynorthwestern.com/2020/05/14/city/ill-drink-to-that-a-history-of-alcohol-and-temperance-in-evanston.

Gale, Neal, PhD. Digital Research Library of Illinois History. drloihjournal.blogspot.com.

GlobeNewswire. "First Busey Corporation Finalizes Acquisition of Cummins-American Corp. and Glenview State Bank." June 2, 2021. www.globenewswire.com/news-release/2021/06/02/2240840/1071/en/First-Busey-Finalizes-Acquisition-of-Cummins-American-Corp-and-Glenview-State-Bank.html.

Gouldsbury, Eric. Email to the author, June 18, 2021.

Grossman, Ron. "In 1962, Chicago Mob Boss Had Sinatra Singing His Way." *Chicago Tribune*, December 6, 2015, 25.

"Hard Times in Illinois, 1930–1940." www.cyberdriveillinois.com.

Hines, Nick. "How Jewish Bootleggers Saved the Day during Prohibition." January 5, 2017. vinepair.com.

Hoynes, Jerome, et al. "New Trier Township 1850–2010, Honoring Our Past; Looking Forward into Our Future, 1850–2010." newtriertownship.com/document/center/View/150/History-Book-PDF.

Jacoby, John. "Hackney's Story Involves Wilmette, Prohibition." *Wilmette Life*, 2013.

Jones, Thom L. Gangsters Inc. www.gangstersinc.org.

Kelly, Debra. "What It Was Really Like Being a Bootlegger during Prohibition." Grunge, May 26, 2021. www.grunge.com/417658/what-it-was-really-like-being-a-bootlegger-during-prohibition.

Klein, Christopher. "A Brief History of Presidential Drinking." History, September 3, 2018. www.history.com/news/a-brief-history-of-presidential-drinking.

———. "The False Armistice Report That Fooled America." History, November 7, 2018. www.history.com/news/false-armistice-report-world-war-i-early-celebration.

———. "FDR Legalizes Sale of Beer and Wine." History, December 10, 2018. www.history.com/this-day-in-history/fdr-legalizes-sale-of-beer-and-wine.

———. "How Prohibition Gave Birth to Nascar." History, August 29, 2018. www.history.com/news/how-prohibition-gave-birth-to-nascar.

Kogan, Rick. "For 70 Years, Meier's Tavern Has Been a Great Suburban Oasis." Chicago Tribune, March 14, 2004. www.chicagotribune.com/news/ct-xpm-2004-03-14-0403130313-story.html.

Kwedar, Melinda Fish. "Inns and Taverns in the Midwest." Sangamon State University. www.ideals.illinois.edu/handle/2142/15419.

Macushla. "Our Story." www.macushlabeer.com/our-story.

Maine, an Encyclopedia. "Alcohol." maineanencyclopedia.com/alcohol.

Markey, Gene. "If I May So." Chicagoan, September 10, 1927. Reproduced by Neil Harris. The Chicagoan, a Lost Magazine of the Jazz Age. Chicago: University of Chicago Press, 2008, 256.

McElroy, Ryan. "The Story of How Moonshiners Created the Performance Car." November 16, 2015. www.carkeys.co.uk/news/the-story-of-how-moonshiners-created-the-performance-car.

McIntyre, Barbara K., and Robert L. McIntyre. "Wheeling through the Years: An Oral History of Wheeling, an Illinois Village." Wheeling Historical Society, June 1, 1987. www.wheelinghistoricalsociety.com/album0/history1.htm.

McKenna, Amy. "Carry Nation." Encyclopedia Britannica. britannica.com/biography/carry-nation.

Meier's Tavern. meierstavern.com.

Mejia, Paula. "The Lucrative Business of Prescribing Booze During Prohibition." Atlas Obscura, November 15, 2017. www.atlasobscura.com.

Mob Museum. "Bootleggers and Bathtub Gin." themobmuseum.org.

New Yorker. "A Bootlegger's Story I. How I Started." September 25, 1926. www.newyorker.com/archive/1926_09_25_025-TNY_CARDS_000166421.

North Shore Magazine. "1933 Meier's Tavern." June 2007.

Northwestern. "Northwestern University History." northwestern.edu/about/history.html.

Ohio History Central. "Temperance Movement." ohiohistorycentral.org/w/temperance_movement.

Okrent, Daniel. "Wayne B. Wheeler: The Man Who Turned Off the Taps." *Smithsonian Magazine*, May 2010. smithsonianmag.org.

Roos, Dave. "How Prohibition Put the 'Organized' in Organized Crime." History, March 9, 2019. www.history.com/news/prohibition-organized-crime-al-capone.

Russell, Daniel. "The Road House: A Study of Commercialized Amusements in the Environs of Chicago." Master's thesis, University of Chicago, 1931.

Sadin, Steve. "Hackney's Shines Rich in Food, History." *Daily North Shore*, March 10, 2019. jwcdaily.com/2016/03/10/glenviews-hackneys-shines-rich-in-food-history.

Schmidt, Elizabeth. "On the Road to Women's Suffrage: The Home Protection Ballot." Evanston Women's History Project at the Evanston History Center, January 24, 2020. suffrage2020illinois.org/2020/01/24/on-the-road-to-womens-suffrage-the-home-protection-ballot.

Schneider, Richard L. Information on Matthew Hoffman. Des Plaines History Center, Des Plaines, IL. Courtesy of George R. Pinkowski and John Binder.

Silsbee, Kirk. "This Hotel Kept All the Secrets of the Rich and Famous…Until Now." *GQ UK*, June 23, 2015. www.gq-magazine.co.uk.

Smith, James. "Reuters and the False Armistice of 7 November 1918." The Baron, April 6, 2017. thebaron.info/archives/reuters-and-the-false-armistice-of-7-november-1918.

Stack, Martin. "A Concise History of America's Brewing Industry." EH.net, July 4, 2003. eh.net/encyclopedia/a-concise-history-of-americas-brewing-industry.

Sutcliffe, Theodora. "Benjamin Franklin." Difford's Guide. diffordsguide.com/encyclopedia/2868/people/benjamin-franklin.

Teeter, Adam. "How Wine Bricks Saved the U.S. Wine Industry during Prohibition." Vine Pair, August 24, 2015. vinepair.com/wine-blog/how-wine-bricks-saved-the-u-s-wine-industry-during-prohibition.

Thompson, Helen. "Meet the Doctor Who Convinced America to Sober Up." *Smithsonian Magazine*, July 6, 2015. www.smithsonianmag.com/smart-news/how-colonial-doctor-changed-medical-views-alcohol-180955813.

Thrillist. "Hackney's." www.thrillist.com/venue/eat/chicago/restaurants/hackneys.

Time. "Prohibition: Wine Bricks." August 17, 1931. content.time.com/time/subscriber/article/0,33009,742105,00.html.

University of Illinois–Urbana-Champaign. illinois.edu/research.

Westerville Public Library. "Why Westerville?" www.westervillelibrary.org/antisaloon-why-westerville.

White, Clare. "Alcohol as Medicine and Poison." prohibition.themobmuseum.org/the-history/the-prohibition-underworld/alcohol-as-medicine-and-poison.

Wikipedia. "Anti-Saloon League." en.wikipedia.org/wiki/Anti-Saloon_League.

———. "Bugs Moran." en.wikipedia.org/wiki/Bugs_Moran.

———. "Frances Willard." en.wikipedia.org/wiki/Frances_Willard.

———. "Johnny Torrio." en.wikipedia.org/wiki/Johnny_Torrio.

———. "1932 United States Presidential Election." en.wikipedia.org/wiki/1932_United_States_presidential_election.

———. "Roger Touhy." en.wikipedia.org/wiki/Roger_Tuohy.

———. "Rum-running." en.wikipedia.org/wiki/Rum-running.

———. "Wayne Wheeler." en.wikipedia.org/wiki/Wayne_Wheeler.

"World War 1 Casualties." www.100letprve.si/en/world_war_1/casualties/index.html.

Zeldes, Leah A. "Hackney's." Dining Chicago. Diningchicago.com.

Newspapers

Arlington Heights Herald. newspapers.com.

Chicago Daily Journal and Public (Clinton, IL). newspapers.com.

Chicago Tribune. newspapers.com.

Daily Chronicle (DeKalb, IL). newspapers.com.

Daily Herald (Chicago). newspapers.com.

Daily Republican-Register (Mount Carmel, IL). newspapers.com.

Glenview Announcements. Glenview Public Library.

Glenview View. Glenview Public Library.

Greater Niles Center News. newspapers.com.

Illinois Issue (Downers Grove, IL). Wilmette Historical Museum.

Journal Gazette (Mattoon, IL). newspapers.com.

Lake Shore News (Wilmette, IL). Wilmette Public Library and Wilmette Historical Museum.

Local News (Wilmette, IL). Wilmette Public Library and Wilmette Historical Museum.

Niles Center Press. Glenview Public Library.

Republican-Northwestern (Belvidere, IL). newspapers.com.

The Times (Streator, IL). newspapers.com

Triblocal.com.

Waukegan News-Sun (Waukegan, IL). newspapers.com.

Wilmette Life. Wilmette Public Library and Wilmette Historical Museum.

Films and Screenplays

Burns, Ken. *Prohibition*. PBS, 2011. 5h 30m. kenburns.com/film/prohibition.

Coppola, Francis Ford. *The Godfather*. Paramount Pictures, 1972. 2h 57m.

Corman, Roger. *The St. Valentine's Day Massacre*. Los Altos, Inc., 1967. 1h 42m.

Faragoh, Francis Edwards. *Little Caesar*. Wisconsin/Warner Bros. Screenplay series, published for the Wisconsin Center for Film and Theater Research by the University of Wisconsin Press, Madison, WI. Copyright 1981, Board of Regents of the University of Wisconsin System.

LeRoy, Mervyn. *Little Caesar*. Warner Bros., 1931. 1h 19m.

Thew, Harvey. *The Public Enemy*, screenplay. Wisconsin/Warner Bros. Screenplay series, published for the Wisconsin Center for Film and Theater Research by the University of Wisconsin Press, Madison, WI, Copyright 1981, Board of Regents of the University of Wisconsin System.

Walsh, Raoul. *The Roaring Twenties*. Warner Bros., 1939. 1h 46m.

Wellmar, William A. *The Public Enemy*. Warner Bros., 1931. 1h 13m.

ABOUT THE AUTHOR

Growing up, Jill Ruschli Crane was fascinated by family tales about the Roaring Twenties in Glenview. As the offspring of bootleggers, bartenders and a gangster's moll, she researched what it was really like in those dry days. Her scrutiny uncovered humble, hardworking people caught up in the Prohibition culture they didn't want as they coped with a frantic time. Her previous endeavors include raising over $1 million for a children's hospital, golfing her way to an 18 handicap (that lasted two weeks) and using her passion for history to author a country club centennial musical review. This is her first book, but more Glenview history is on its way with her next book about Curtiss-Reynolds Airfield, Glenview's premier airport, the precursor to the Glenview Naval Air Station.